Using Innovative Methods in Early Years Research

G000070670

Exploring a range of unconventional research methods and considering how these can be used effectively in practice, this accessible textbook encourages the use of innovative approaches to conduct research in early years contexts.

Using Innovative Methods in Early Years Research provides key information on a range of non-traditional research methods, and details the strengths, limitations and challenges involved in diverging from more standard research methods. From researching with young children, practitioners and parents, to harnessing the arts, vignettes, identity boxes and narrative accounts, chapters draw on authors' first-hand experiences to highlight the value of 'thinking outside the box' and developing innovative research methods that meet the needs and aims of the researcher, while also involving and empowering research participants. Including detailed information on ethical concerns and the importance of reflexivity, individual and group tasks encourage students to take a critical and well-thought-out approach to conducting independent research.

This will be an invaluable and inspiring resource for high-level undergraduate and postgraduate students as they embark on research projects in the field of early years education and care.

Zeta Brown is Reader in Education for Social Justice at the University of Wolverhampton, UK.

Helen Perkins is Senior Lecturer in Childhood and Family Studies at the University of Wolverhampton, UK.

Using Innovative Methods in Early Years Research

Beyond the Conventional

Edited by Zeta Brown and Helen Perkins

Routledge
Taylor & Francis Group

LONDON AND NEW YORK

First published 2019
by Routledge
2 Park Square, Milton Park, Abingdon, Oxon OX14 4RN

and by Routledge
52 Vanderbilt Avenue, New York, NY 10017

Routledge is an imprint of the Taylor & Francis Group, an informa business

© 2019 selection and editorial matter, Zeta Brown and Helen Perkins; individual chapters, the contributors

The right of Zeta Brown and Helen Perkins to be identified as the authors of the editorial material, and of the authors for their individual chapters, has been asserted in accordance with sections 77 and 78 of the Copyright, Designs and Patents Act 1988.

All rights reserved. No part of this book may be reprinted or reproduced or utilised in any form or by any electronic, mechanical, or other means, now known or hereafter invented, including photocopying and recording, or in any information storage or retrieval system, without permission in writing from the publishers.

Trademark notice: Product or corporate names may be trademarks or registered trademarks, and are used only for identification and explanation without intent to infringe.

British Library Cataloguing-in-Publication Data
A catalogue record for this book is available from the British Library

Library of Congress Cataloging-in-Publication Data
Names: Brown, Zeta, editor. | Perkins, Helen (Helen Marie), 1957- editor.
Title: Using innovative methods in early years research : beyond the
    conventional / edited by Zeta Brown and Helen Perkins.
Description: Abingdon, Oxon ; New York, NY : Routledge, 2019. |
    Includes bibliographical references and index.
Identifiers: LCCN 2019001902 (print) | LCCN 2019009883 (ebook) | ISBN
    9780429423871 (eb) | ISBN 9781138389502 (hbk. : alk. paper) | ISBN
    9781138389519 (pbk. : alk. paper) | ISBN 9780429423871 (ebook)
Subjects: LCSH: Early childhood education—Research—Methodology.
Classification: LCC LB1139.225 (ebook) | LCC LB1139.225 .U75 2019
    (print) | DDC 372.21—dc23
LC record available at https://lccn.loc.gov/2019001902

ISBN: 978-1-138-38950-2 (hbk)
ISBN: 978-1-138-38951-9 (pbk)
ISBN: 978-0-429-42387-1 (ebk)

Typeset in Melior
by Swales & Willis Ltd, Exeter, Devon, UK

Zeta Brown

For my amazing children: Mia, Damie and Fin

And my very supportive parents: Sue and John

Helen Perkins

For my wonderfully supportive husband Rob and my children Fiona and James

Contents

Abbreviations

BA	Bachelor of Arts
BEEL	baby effective early learning
BERA	British Education Research Association
BESA	British Education Studies Association
CATE	Collaborative Award for Teaching Excellence
CREC	Centre for Research in Early Childhood
DfE	Department for Education
ECE	early childhood education
ECEC	early childhood education and care
ECS	early childhood studies
EECERA	European Early Childhood Education Research Association
EEL	Effective Early Learning Project
EYPP	Early Years Pupil Premium
FE	further education
GB	Gigabyte
GCSE	General Certificate of Secondary Education
GDPR	General Data Protection Regulation
HE	higher education
HEA	Higher Education Academy
ICT	information and communications technology
ITET	Initial Teacher Education or Training
LA	local authority
LOtC	learning outside of the classroom
PE	physical education
PVI	Private, Voluntary and Independent

REDO	reveal, examine, dismantle, open
SEN	special educational needs
SIG	special interest group
UCL	University College London
UK	United Kingdom
UNCRC	United Nations Convention on the Rights of the Child

Figures

Contributors

Dylan Adams is a Lecturer in Primary Education Studies at Cardiff Metropolitan University. He was a primary school teacher for 13 years before becoming an educational consultant. He is currently undertaking a PhD. His research is focused on constructing a framework of music literacy based on children's experiences of making music in outdoor rural environments.

Gary Beauchamp is Professor of Education and Associate Dean (Research) in the School of Education at Cardiff Metropolitan University. He worked for many years as a primary school teacher before moving into higher education, where he has led undergraduate and postgraduate courses in education, as well as supervising doctoral students. His research interests focus on ICT in education, particularly the use of interactive technologies in learning and teaching. He has published widely in academic journals, as well as writing books, book chapters and research reports, and is a member of the BERA Council. In addition, he has been an additional inspector for Estyn, a chair of governors in two primary schools, and has served as external examiner for many universities.

Elisabetta Biffi is a Researcher in Pedagogy at the Department of Human Sciences for Education "Riccardo Massa" – University of Milano-Bicocca. She has been in this post since 2010, and teaches on 'Narrative Theories and Practices' on the master's degree course of Educational Sciences. She is a member of national and European research projects on the topics of pedagogical documentation, childhood protection and children's rights, and educators' and teachers' professional development. She is a member of different editorial boards, including the press board of *Encyclopaideia: Journal of Phenomenology and Education*. She is also a member of education associations, including the EECERA, where she is co-convenor for the SIG 'Transforming Assessment, Evaluation and Documentation in Early Childhood Pedagogy'.

Zeta Brown is Reader in Education for Social Justice at the University of Wolverhampton, England, and is leader of the 'Children, Young People and Families' research cluster for the university's Education Observatory. She is an executive member and currently chair of the British Education Studies Association (BESA). Zeta's research predominantly focuses on agendas and policies in early and primary education.

Sandra Dumitrescu is a Lecturer in Early Childhood Studies at Cardiff Metropolitan University. Sandra is interested in play from a rights-based perspective, for those children with complex and profound needs. This has developed from practice, having previously been a practitioner within children's palliative care.

Cheryl Ellis is a Principal Lecturer and Head of Department within the School of Education and Social Policy at Cardiff Metropolitan University. She is a member of the university's outdoor learning team and regularly works with children and students within Forest School. Her key areas of research interest include outdoor learning and play, inclusion, and additional learning needs. Having previously worked as a primary school teacher, Cheryl has experienced the 'practical realities' of classroom life.

Chantelle Haughton is Senior Lecturer in Early Childhood Studies at Cardiff Metropolitan University. Also a Forest School leader and trainer, she pioneered and developed an outdoor learning centre on campus, generating use of a strip of ancient Welsh woodland, a concrete 'patch' and the building of a charity-funded log cabin. Chantelle was awarded the Student Led Teaching Fellowship Award (2013) and the Vice-Chancellor's Award for Excellence (2011), and was an HEA CATE finalist (2018). These awards were related to playful community engagement projects that involve students, local children and practitioners as partners.

Laura Heads is completing her doctoral studies at Northumbria University, exploring the perspectives of reception children in the 'school readiness' debate. As part of this project, Laura has endeavoured to use a creative methodology to capture moments of children's creativity and intelligence. Laura's interest in early years research has been shaped by her experiences as a primary school and early years teacher. Future aspirations include working more closely with undergraduate and postgraduate students to inspire them to think differently about young children and more critically about education.

Kieran Hodgkin is a Senior Lecturer in Education Studies within the School of Education and Social Policy at Cardiff Metropolitan University. Kieran completed his PhD in July 2014. His research centred on pupils' expectations and experiences of the primary–secondary transition, with a specific focus on physical education (PE). Kieran is currently chair of the school's ethics committee and programme director for the undergraduate Education Studies/Primary Education Studies programme.

Sarah Holmes is Postdoctoral Teaching Fellow in Early Childhood at Liverpool Hope University. Her research interests include holistic well-being of young children, the influence of family, children's spirituality, and the impact of religion on children. Alongside this, Sarah is involved in various school and community-based voluntary projects working among children aged 2 to 12 years old. She also has three children of her own, who bring great joy and provide significant insight into the early years.

Michael Jopling is Professor of Education and Director of the Education Observatory in the Institute of Education at the University of Wolverhampton. He has been involved in research in all areas of education, using a range of methods and approaches, but his research interests and publications centre on school collaboration, multi-agency support for vulnerable groups, education policy and leadership, and how to engage teachers and practitioners in research and enquiry.

Zenna Kingdon is a Senior Lecturer at the University of Wolverhampton, with expertise in preschool education, primary education and pedagogic theory. Her research interests focus on play, and in particular role play, and exploring the concept of flourishing in early childhood.

Helen Lyndon is the Postgraduate Programme Lead for the Centre for Research in Early Childhood (CREC) in Birmingham. She taught initially in primary school education, specialising in mathematics, then undertook a master's degree in Early Years Education while teaching in children's centres. She went on to work in higher education on undergraduate and postgraduate courses relating to early childhood education. Her doctoral research, almost complete, focuses on pedagogic mediation, including development of listening methods for daily practice with young children. Helen is the UK Country Coordinator for the European Early Childhood Education Research Association (EECERA).

Jackie Musgrave is Programme Lead for Early Childhood and Education Studies (Primary) at the Open University. Her research brings together her experiences as a Registered Sick Children's Nurse and as a teacher of early childhood. The focus of her research is to identify the role of practitioners in reducing or removing the barriers that health matters can create for very young children, and in creating inclusive education and care environments for such children. Her two chapters in this book are drawn from her doctoral research.

Ioanna Palaiologou is an Academic Associate of the UCL Institute of Education and a child psychologist. Her research in early childhood focuses on ethics, child development, leadership and implications for pedagogy, and the role of technology in children's lives. She was awarded best published paper for 2017 in the *European Early Childhood Education Research Journal* for her article 'Children under Five and Digital Technologies: Implications for Early Years Pedagogy'.

Helen Perkins is Senior Lecturer in Childhood and Family Studies at the University of Wolverhampton. She began her early years career working in nursery and reception. Following 13 years as head of school for early childhood education in a college of further and higher education, Helen joined the University of Wolverhampton as a senior lecturer working on undergraduate and postgraduate courses. Helen's doctoral research predominantly focuses on agendas and policies in the early years, with a focus on the workforce and their qualifications. Helen served as an expert panel member for the Nutbrown Review of early years qualifications, and is a member of the Executive for the Early Childhood Studies Degree Network, focusing on workforce issues and professionalism.

Gavin Rhoades is a Principal Lecturer and Head of Student Transitions in the Faculty of Education, Health and Wellbeing at the University of Wolverhampton. Prior to joining the university, he was an assistant head teacher at secondary schools in Staffordshire and Cumbria. His research interests, including his current doctoral study, are focused on issues around student satisfaction and retention in higher education.

Lynn Richards, now retired, previously taught for 12 years on undergraduate programmes within the discipline of early childhood, family and community at the University of Wolverhampton. Her professional background is in working with children, young people and their families in a variety of provisions: early years settings, play schemes, youth clubs and community projects. Highlighting the need for person-centred working, her professional doctorate in Education focused on student articulations of belonging and the affective dimension of teaching-learning.

Siân Sarwar is a Lecturer in Early Childhood Studies at Cardiff Metropolitan University. Her research interests include music education, creativity and informal learning, and children's rights within education (particularly in relation to children's participation). Siân has worked as a musician and secondary school music teacher and taught on the BA Secondary Music ITET programme at Cardiff Metropolitan University. She was also Project Officer for Musical Futures Wales. She is currently working towards her PhD, exploring children's participation in music.

Jacky Tyrie is a Lecturer in the early childhood studies (ECS) team at Cardiff Metropolitan University. Having completed her PhD in 2010, examining children's access to their rights in Wales and the impact of gender on access to rights, she has since developed these focuses in a range of research projects. Jacky is currently exploring ways of examining young children's 'lived' experiences of human rights.

Franca Zuccoli is an Associated Professor and Lecturer at the Department of Human Sciences for Education "Riccardo Massa" – University of Milano-Bicocca, where she teaches 'Teaching and Learning Didactics' and 'Art Education' on the master's degree course of Teacher Education. She is a member of the orientation committee at the University of Milano-Bicocca, with special responsibility for "Riccardo Massa" Department of Educational Human Sciences.

Introduction

Zeta Brown and Helen Perkins

Our main aim for this book was to provide students with a resource that offers unconventional, innovative research methods that can be used in early childhood education. Many early childhood education studies successfully use traditional research methods, such as interviews and questionnaires. However, thinking 'outside the box' can provide researchers with methods that access participants' perspectives in differing ways. In our experience, the use of unconventional research methods can provide unique findings that may not have been apparent if the researcher had decided to use traditional research methods.

The book is structured in three parts. Part I focuses on researching in early childhood education and provides readers with some of the essential wider considerations they need to know when using innovative research methods. For example, in Chapter 1 Musgrave examines how reflexivity has become an essential ingredient in high-quality educational research, and in Chapter 2 Hodgkin and Beauchamp consider the ethical challenges researchers face when employing innovative methods. Part II focuses on unconventional research methods that involve research with children. For instance, in Chapter 4 Biffi and Zuccoli focus on arts as a research method to investigate children's thinking and educational experiences, and in Chapter 10 Palaiologou focuses on the use of vignettes in research with young children. Part III is focused on unconventional research methods that can be used in research with practitioners and parents. For example, in Chapter 12 Richards demonstrates how narrative inquiry can be used with student-practitioners to foreground the voice of participants.

The book's target audience is level 6–8 early childhood studies students who are studying an undergraduate degree, master's programme or doctorate. However, its content is also relevant for students studying related courses in areas including education studies and family and community studies. We wanted to ensure that this book was accessible to undergraduate and postgraduate students. This is because unconventional, innovative research methods are often reserved for resources aimed at postgraduate students. In this book, all research methods can be used (subject to ethical and supervisory approval) in level 6–8 studies.

It was important to us that all chapters included at least one reflection on a study that used each detailed research method. Many of the contributors reflected on innovative methods used in their doctoral studies. These included Kingdon, in Chapter 8, who detailed her adapted use of the mosaic approach as an ethnographic methodology. In Chapter 11, Perkins also describes how she developed the use of identity boxes as a research method that she used in her doctoral studies, and in Chapter 13 Musgrave details how her use of observations afforded her the opportunity of gaining rich data that helped her learn about what was important for her participant.

There is an overarching theme in this book that is included in most of the chapters and also the part titles of the book. Contributors detail the need to empower participants (adults and young children) so that research is done 'with' and not 'on' them. Some of the chapters that detail the involvement of participants in data collection include Chapter 6 by Heads and Jopling. This chapter details the importance of working with and listening to children during messy, playful research. In Chapter 7, Holmes discusses how play-based interview techniques can be used to discover children's thoughts, feelings and ideas. In Chapter 9, Beauchamp et al. also detail the importance of using a multimodal approach (such as videos) that can enable children to collect their own data and evidence their views of the world and their interactions in it. In Chapter 14, Brown and Rhoades also discuss the importance of providing subjectivity to participants when using Q-methodology. This is to ensure the participants conduct the measurements, instead of being subjected to measurement.

The involvement of participants in this way led to detailed discussions in some of the chapters around ethics. For instance, in Chapter 3 Palaiologou ethically questions the role of the adult in participatory research. We decided early on in the planning process that we needed a chapter dedicated to ethics. This is Chapter 2, which has been written by Hodgkin and Beauchamp. The key concerns mentioned in this chapter can also be found in relation to specific research methods throughout the book. For instance, Hodgkin and Beauchamp discuss the need to involve young children in consent/assent. In Chapter 5, Lyndon also mentions consent/assent in relation to the use of drawing methods with young children. These contributors state that it is important that consent/assent is monitored. Children should be able to leave the data collection at any point and should not feel 'compelled' to complete the activity.

Overall, this book has uniquely brought together contributors, including noted and international academics that have practically used the detailed research methods. By bringing these individuals together in one book, readers are able to reflect on their position as a researcher and select chapters that they would like to consider further for their own data collection.

In this field, 'early years education' and 'early childhood, education and care' are synonymously used to describe the education of children from birth to 8 years old. The 'early years' is a recognised term in in UK practice. However, in the book's content, we have attempted to move this terminology on to more contemporary terms such as early childhood, early childhood, and care and early education in order to bridge theory and practice.

INDIVIDUAL/GROUP TASK

When planning your own research project, it is important to consider whether you have time, particularly in a small-scale study, for the detailed preparation required when using innovative and creative methods. Take a moment here to reflect on the size and scale of your own study. How many participants are involved in your study? What is the timescale for submitting your study? What access do you have to resources? What kind of data would you like to collect? And finally, what are your reasons/justification for considering using an unconventional methodology?

PART I

Research in early education

Reflexivity in educational research

Jackie Musgrave

Introduction

This chapter begins by examining how reflexivity has become an essential ingredient in high-quality educational research. It explores a range of definitions of reflexivity in qualitative educational research, drawing on peer-reviewed journal articles to illustrate how reflexivity is addressed in the literature. The content identifies the factors that inform and shape our beliefs, and in turn our motivation for conducting our research. A central argument is that our research is 'not a voyage of discovery that starts with a clean sheet' (Denscombe, 2007: 68). The reasons why it is imperative to acknowledge and lay bare our motivations and reflexivity are foregrounded, helping the reader to be aware that it is impossible and unnecessary to be objective, and in fact it can be unethical not to explore and declare our reflexivity in relation to our research. The skills necessary to be reflexive are also discussed, such as the ability to be critically reflective, especially in relation to the possible impact our research may have on others. Examples of how I used Brookfield's lenses to achieve this in my doctoral thesis are included (Musgrave, 2014). The chapter also acknowledges that reflexivity can be a painful process when the subject of our research is deeply personal. An aim of the chapter is to support the researcher to navigate the line between excessive or indulgent self-reflection (i.e. 'navel-gazing'), but instead giving guidance about getting the tone right when writing about one's reflexivity. The chapter concludes by emphasising that reflexivity is an essential ingredient of high-quality early childhood educational research.

Reflexivity in qualitative research

Until the middle of the last century, researchers were divided into those who used quantitative and those who used qualitative paradigms. Indeed, Wellington et al. (2005) suggest that such polarisation between the two paradigms still exists, pointing out that the qualitative/quantitative dichotomy is artificial and unhelpful. Such was the strength of feeling among academics about the merits of the two approaches that there were heated 'discussions' about their value to research. In brief, quantitative research was seen as being scientific, robust and objective, whereas qualitative research was seen as being subjective, less robust and less trustworthy. Part of the 'problem' with qualitative research, from the advocates of the use of quantitative data, was that issues were explored in greater depth, using smaller numbers of human participants.

Qualitative data explored the stories behind the numbers that were gathered in quantitative data. The tension between advocates of quantitative or qualitative research was partly based on the historical need to be objective and scientific when presenting findings. As approaches to qualitative research developed, there was a realisation that researchers needed to ask questions that were meaningful to them. When a researcher has a deep interest in a research question, it can reduce the objectivity, or, as Denscombe (2007) puts it, 'what chance is there that the research will provide a fair and balanced picture?' (p. 5). Research that is close to our hearts means that there is undoubtedly and understandably a bias and lack of objectivity; our interests inevitably mean that we are subjective about our research. This may mean that bias may be difficult to remove from the research. Consequently, as qualitative research has emerged and matured, there is a realisation that such subjectivity, defined as 'the quality of being influenced or informed by one's own opinion', should be recognised and explored as part of the methodology of research (Oates, 2018). The process of examining one's motivation for pursuing our chosen research is referred to as *reflexivity*.

Defining reflexivity

There are a number of different definitions of the concept of reflexivity; however, it would appear that academics who have offered their interpretation are united in agreement that reflexivity is to do with self-awareness. This means that there is a need to be self-aware about the motivations for focusing on the area of research. It is important to differentiate between a similar term that is used in qualitative research (i.e. *reflectivity*), which is defined by Oates (2018) as 'the act of applying critical evaluative thinking to one's behaviour. In research, seeking to become aware of potential personal biases or shortcomings in all stages and aspects of research'. While the use of reflectivity is important in research, Oates (2018) distinguishes reflectivity from reflexivity:

> In research, reflexivity refers to a researcher applying to themselves the same critical frame, methods or analyses that they apply to their research topic, participants and data. For example, a discourse analyst might reflexively analyse their own discursive treatment of their data. Commonly erroneously used interchangeably with 'reflectivity'.

Therefore, one can see that, as Oleson (2005) suggests, 'reflexivity goes beyond mere reflection, it demands a steady and uncomfortable assessment of the interpersonal and interstitial knowledge' (p. 251). Reflexivity is to do with examining how the self is part of the account of the research. It requires, as Punch (2003) states, 'constant reflection on the social processes and the personal characteristics and values of the researcher which inform the data generated as well as the subsequent interpretation and data analysis' (p. 97). This implies that applying reflexivity is a thread that runs through each aspect of the research process.

How 'to do' reflexivity

As researchers, we can 'do' reflexivity (i.e. by isolating the focus of our research and asking critical questions of ourselves so that we can capture the reasons why our research is important to us). Therefore, the process of applying reflexivity to your research requires you to closely examine your motivations for choosing the research. Wellington et al. (2005), in a book aimed at doctoral students, suggests that examination of our motives starts with examining our life history. He and his colleagues created a framework for a personal life history, which is a list of questions that are designed to provoke reflection on students' lives. The questions ask for information that covers personal information about family, experience of childhood, educational experience, occupations, personal relationships, and interests and pursuits. Such questions are designed to encourage deep reflection of not only the chronology of lives, but examination of how and why events may have initiated feelings about or developed our interest in a certain issue. Wellington et al. (2005) claim that examining our life history in this way and acknowledging our motivations is a vital part of the process because our 'life history can't be compartmentalised' (p. 20), meaning that we cannot suspend our beliefs, separate our experience or delete our memories because our experiences will be inextricably linked with how we view and analyse the data we collect during our research.

INDIVIDUAL TASK

As Wellington et al. (2005) state, there is no 'right way' to do a life history; they suggest that a timeline using a chronological approach can be helpful. The following task is based on their framework for a personal life history:

1. Consider your life history. Start with your place and date of birth, and write down details about the context of your life to include family and your childhood, experience of education, community and context, and personal relationships.

2. When you have completed part 1, consider how the life events and the attitudes and beliefs of your family and community shaped you. How did gender, social class, ethnicity and sexuality influence who you are?

3. Does any of this information help to shine a light on why you are interested in your area of research?

Using reflexivity in my research

When I had reached the point in my doctoral research where I felt that I had a research focus and had started to plan my questions, I realised that I needed to critically reflect on my reasons for feeling so drawn to this focus. My research question was: *How do practitioners create inclusive environments for young children with chronic health conditions?* As I reflected on the reasons for the origins of my research, I experienced an 'aha' moment (i.e. a critical event that contributed to my reasons for choosing this research focus). As a teacher of early childhood studies students, I had been visiting nursery settings to carry out visits to students on placements. While there, I noticed that several young children had eczema; the angry patches of inflamed skin were very evident, especially on their hands and faces and in the folds of their arms. The word 'eczema' is derived from the Greek word meaning 'to boil' because the discomfort of this skin condition is akin to the pain caused by the skin being boiled. One 6-month-old baby was so itchy because of the eczema patches that he would rub his cheek against the fabric of the baby rocker in order to relieve the itch. He would also use his nails to scratch the patches on his arms, scratching with such vigour that he would make himself bleed. Such was the intensity of his scratching that the practitioners had put socks on his hands to stop him from scratching. The only time that the gloves were removed was when his key person could sit with him for one-to-one interaction, where she would distract him from thinking about the constant itch and his need to scratch to relieve the pain and discomfort. The practitioner used toys and talked and sang to him so that his attention was diverted. I remember thinking to myself: I wonder if wearing the socks on his hands is interfering with his fine motor skill development? How does he feel when he gets an itch on a part of his body that he can't reach to scratch and relieve the itch? I realised that I was particularly drawn to this baby and the ways that the eczema was interfering with his life, and I was aware that he relied on his key person's knowledge and understanding about him and how eczema affected him. I realised that I wanted to explore how practitioners had developed inclusive practice for children with common chronic health conditions such as eczema. Although this incident is critical and vividly etched on my memory, I was aware that there were other motivations for my interest in this area of research that needed to be explored and articulated.

Exploring motivations for my research focus

Cannella and Lincoln (2007) remind us that part of becoming an ethical researcher requires the researcher to ask, 'How do I assemble myself as an ethical researcher?' (p. 326). I became aware that a starting point in assembling myself as an ethical researcher began as I identified my reflexivity in relation to my research. My interest in the research question is informed by professional and personal interest. Ely (1991, cited in Possick, 2009) suggests that research projects are interwoven with the researcher's deepest social and professional passions and commitments.

Considering other personal and professional perspectives

Having reflected on my personal life history earlier, I realised that being reflexive needed me to not just take a linear and chronological approach to examine my life history, but also to examine my life history from the different roles (i.e. the perspectives) that had influenced my choice of research. However, the differing perspectives were interwoven, and I needed a framework that would help me to critique the reasons why these different perspectives had influenced my research. I realised that adapting an approach similar to that of Brookfield's (1995) lenses would help me to examine each part of my life through a different lens. By separating out each part of my biography, I could shine a light on the influences and reasons why my research was so important (see Figure 1.1).

Adapting Brookfield's lenses

Brookfield (1995) highlighted the importance of extending our reflection and becoming critical reflectors. Being critical does not entail just being negative, although it is important to examine the 'cons' as well as the 'pros'. In order to be a critical reflector, Brookfield (1995) suggests that we use different 'lenses' in order to look at an issue from a different perspective or vantage point. The analogy is that in the same way a pair of spectacles with prescription lenses will help an individual to see the world clearly, in a similar way, by looking down a specific lens, we can consider issues from another's perspective. In relation to conducting research with children, it is vital to develop the ability to attempt to look at the world from their perspective, in order to be able to listen to them and to be able to identify ways of sharing power and agency.

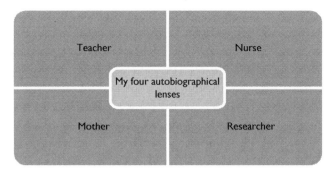

Figure 1.1 Using Brookfield's autobiographical lenses to explore reflexivity

Having identified the four autobiographical lenses through which to view my research, I used critical questions, asking why, where, when, how, who and what to identify how my experiences had brought me to my research focus. One example is that I was able to draw on my knowledge of chronic health conditions that I had gained as a nurse and the experience gained as a mother of a child with a number of chronic health conditions. To illustrate this point, my daughter had severe eczema on her hands, which sometimes became infected, and this caused her pain and caused me as her mother to be anxious about her well-being.

As a nurse, I was aware that infected eczema is very unpleasant and potentially life-threatening. As a teacher of early childhood students, I learned about the importance of sensory play using a range of different media such as sand, water, shaving foam and mud. However, for children with eczematous hands, engaging with these commonly used resources may provoke painful and unsightly outbreaks of inflammation. Babies and very young children are not necessarily aware that there are specific substances that can provoke outbreaks, so they are likely to engage with the activities and unknowingly suffer the consequences afterwards. I had reflected on the impact of having eczema on one's hands, and was aware that it could be a barrier to participation in messy play activities. This realisation piqued my curiosity and made me wonder what the practitioners did to protect the children from coming into contact with triggers in the early childhood setting. If the babies and young children could not take part in activities because of the symptoms of their chronic health condition, then this meant that they were being excluded from their education.

So, what did the practitioners do in order to remove or minimise the triggers in order to maximise the children's participation?

Drawing on this example from my own research illustrates that without this process of critically reflecting on my previous experience and knowledge that was gained from being a mother of a child with eczema, a teacher of early childhood studies students, and a nurse with a specialist interest in eczema, the justification for my research would not have been as meaningful. However, there could have been a danger of what Sultana (2007) referred to as 'navel-gazing' (a point that will be returned to below) because I could have focused on the perspective of being a mother of a child with eczema, and focused too much on the negative aspects of being a parent of a child with severe eczema. Undoubtedly, this is a situation that can impact on not only the child, but all of the family, because of sleepless nights caused by itchy, painful skin. However, to focus on my own perspective would have taken away from the purpose of my research, which was to explore how practitioners included children with chronic health conditions in their early education. I continued to examine my reflexivity in relation to how my four perspectives could influence what I heard or saw in a way that could challenge the trustworthiness or academic rigour of my findings. I found that capturing my thoughts in a research journal helped me to grapple with these issues.

INDIVIDUAL/GROUP TASK

1. Identify your lenses and consider your research through each lens.

2. Apply the why, where, when, how, who and what questions to examine how your life history and experiences from these perspectives have brought you to your research focus.

Strengths and limitations of reflexivity

Reflexivity in qualitative research is important and can be a strength; however, there are some limitations and words of caution to consider.

A strength of being reflexive is that documenting your life history and critically considering how your life experiences have helped to shape your focus of research helps you to challenge previously held assumptions and beliefs. Being reflexive can move research away from a scientific and calculated interpretation of data towards a highly emotional interpretation of the data, which can mean that it illuminates the humanity of research. However, as with many aspects of learning to be a researcher in higher education, not only is there a new language to learn, but there is also a degree of skill required in how reflexivity is approached. There is a skill in getting the balance right when exploring life events in order to identify what it is that has piqued our curiosity and draws us, or in some cases compels us to explore our area of research. On the one hand, there is a danger of addressing the reflexive motivation in a superficial and ultimately meaningless way. On the other hand, the level of introspection can be such that the researcher can be accused of 'navel-gazing', meaning that, as the metaphor suggests, the researcher becomes focused on one aspect of their positionality and fails to take in the broader perspective. Sultana (2007), while acknowledging that this can be an argument against reflexivity in qualitative research, does not believe that being reflexive about one's positionality is self-indulgent. She counters that *how* we reflect on our position in our research 'influences methods, interpretations and knowledge production' (p. 376). Her points resonated with the reflexivity I engaged with during my research, because I realised that exploring the deeply personal perspectives of my life that had informed my research interest helped enrich my research.

Engaging with research can become part of one's life history. In the same way that life events can become part of one's history, so can the experience of engaging with research. This is especially the case when engaging with a prolonged piece of research (e.g. research linked to a qualification such as a degree). For some researchers, engaging with reflexivity can be a highly emotional experience. By virtue of the fact that engaging with reflexivity can provoke high emotions, this can be a negative experience, and sometimes this may mean that researchers protect themselves from emotional stress (Possick, 2009).

Some guidance about including reflexivity in your research

I found that writing regularly in my research journal helped me to identify the reflexivity for my research. By writing down my thoughts in this way, I found that any content that was deeply emotional was 'safe', meaning it was private to me. When it came to writing the section about reflexivity in my thesis, I was able to adapt my writing and reduce the emotive language. However, it was important to be able to convey the emotional impact that informed my reflexivity. It is important to ensure that your reflexivity is linked to your research question and to articulate the connections in clear and factual language. Considering how you can avoid the possibility of your research causing harm needs careful thought as you explore your reflexivity. In the same way as you consider how you will anonymise details about your participants and also how you maintain confidentiality with your participants, it is vital that you do not reveal details that may identify people, places and events that you refer to. This is especially important if the nature of your reflexivity is sensitive. It is also important to consider how people who read your thesis will be affected by what you write. It is important to be factual, but it may be necessary to soften your language and avoid sounding accusatory or critical about events that have informed your reflexivity. If you are concerned about this aspect of your research, it is a good idea to gain feedback from peers and your research supervisor.

Conclusion

I conclude this chapter by returning to Sultana's (2007) words, where she asserts that 'a reflexive research process can open up the research to more complex and nuanced understandings of issues' (p. 376). Undoubtedly, being reflexive and identifying the perspectives from which I explored my positionality helped me to bring together aspects of my life history so that I was able to bring together the threads of knowledge, experience and understanding of what lay behind the different perspectives of the participants in my research. By acknowledging the reflexive positions, I was able to reduce the 'risks to the trustworthiness of the research and transform threats into opportunities to enrich qualitative data analysis' (Possick, 2009: 859).

Summary

Reflexivity:

■ is an essential 'ingredient' in qualitative research, especially in relation to the ethics of research;

■ requires deep introspection from a range of perspectives from your life history;

■ can be an emotional experience, so it is important to manage your feelings and to seek support if necessary;

■ should avoid 'navel-gazing' (i.e. excessive contemplation of an issue to the extent that other perspectives are not addressed); and

■ should be based on relevance to your research question(s).

Recommended reading

Clough, P. and Nutbrown, C. (2012) *A Student's Guide to Methodology*. London: Sage.

Goodley, D., Lawthom, R., Clough, P. and Moore, M. (2004) *Researching Life Stories: Method, Theory and Analyses in a Biographical Age*. London: RoutledgeFalmer.

Lewis, V., Kellett, M., Robinson, C., Fraser, S. and Ding, S. (2004) *The Reality of Research with Children and Young People*. London: Sage.

Nutbrown, C. (2018) *Early Childhood Educational Research*. London: Sage.

Powell, N., Fitzgerald, R., Taylor, N.J. and Graham, A. (2012) *International Literature Review: Ethical Issues in Undertaking Research with Children and Young People*. Lismore: Southern Cross University, Centre for Children and Young People/Dunedin: University of Otago, Centre for Research on Children and Families.

References

Brookfield, S. (1995) *Becoming a Critically Reflective Teacher*. San Francisco, CA: Jossey-Bass.

Cannella, G.S and Lincoln Y.S. (2007) Predatory vs dialogic ethics: constructing an illusion or ethical practice as the core of research methods. *Qualitative Inquiry*, 13(3): 315–335.

Denscombe, M. (2007) *The Good Research Guide: For Small-Scale Social Research Projects*. Maidenhead: Open University Press.

Musgrave, J. (2014) *How Do Practitioners Create Inclusive Environments for Children with Chronic Health Conditions? An Exploratory Case Study.* PhD thesis, University of Sheffield. Available at: http://etheses.whiterose.ac.uk/6174/1/Jackie%20Musgrave%20-%20Final%20Thesis%20incl%20Access%20Form%20for%20submission%2019-5-14.pdf (accessed 21 September 2018).

Oates, J. (2018) Personal communication via email.

Oleson, V. (2005) Early millennial feminist qualitative research: challenges and contours. In N.K. Denzin and Y.S. Lincoln (eds), *The Sage Handbook of Qualitative Research*, 3rd edn. London: Sage, pp. 235–278.

Possick, C. (2009) Reflexive positioning in a politically sensitive situation: dealing with the threats of researching the west bank settlers experience. *Qualitative Inquiry*, 15(5): 859–875.

Punch, S. (2003) Children's use of space and time in Bolivia. In V. Lewis, M. Kellett, C. Robinson, S. Fraser and S. Ding (eds), *The Reality of Research with Children and Young People*. London: Sage, pp. 115–119.

Sultana, F. (2007) Reflexivity, positionality and participatory ethics: negotiating fieldwork dilemmas in international research. *ACM: An International Journal for Critical Geographies*, 6(3): 374–385. Available at: www.acme-journal.org/index.php/acme/article/view/786 (accessed 21 September 2018).

Wellington, J., Bathmaker, A., Hunt, C., McCulloch, G. and Sikes, P. (2005) *Succeeding with Your Doctorate*. London: Sage.

2

Ethical considerations in using innovative methods in early education research

Kieran Hodgkin and Gary Beauchamp

Introduction

Conducting ethical research, and gaining informed consent from young children, can be challenging in 'normal' research. However, as research methods become more innovative, there is a corresponding need, and challenge, in becoming more agile and innovative in ethical matters. This means that ethical decision-making becomes 'an actively deliberative, ongoing and iterative process of assessing and reassessing the situation and issues as they arise' (BERA, 2018: 2). This chapter will explore how ethical concerns can be addressed to reflect this. In particular, the use of a variety of visual and technological solutions will be explored. More specifically, this will include a consideration of informed consent/assent, appropriate means of gaining each from young people, interpreting and validating results, and the sharing and dissemination of research findings in a variety of forms. This chapter will consider the ethical considerations needed to implement research methods detailed in chapters in this book, with particular attention paid to the complex ethical considerations involved in videoing young people in education.

Informed consent/assent in early education research

The concept of informed consent is closely aligned with the ethical principle of ensuring 'respect for persons' (Brooks et al., 2014). The complexities
surrounding informed consent have troubled researchers for the past few
decades (e.g. Israel and Hay, 2006; Miller and Boulton, 2007), and yet
the notion of informed consent remains fundamentally problematic and
slippery (Aaltonen, 2017). Over the years, gaining *fully* informed consent
has become more formal, standardised and better documented (Aaltonen,
2017). However, the need for greater flexibility in relation to informed
consent, and importantly assent, is more important than ever. Literature
makes a distinction between consent and assent (Bourke and Loveridge,
2014). Coyne (2010) indicates that consent refers to a 'person's voluntary positive agreement whilst assent refers to a person's acquiescence'
(p. 228). Alderson and Morrow (2011) argue that assent is at least not refus-
ing to participate, and this they argue is insufficient grounds for assuming
that a child is agreeing; they may be too afraid or confused to refuse to be
involved. However, the British Education Research Association (BERA)
maintains that 'researchers should fully explore ways in which participants can be supported to participate with assent' (BERA, 2018: 15). In
this complex area, Green (2012) makes the simple distinction between
consent, where adults give permission for themselves or their child, and
assent, where permission is given by the child.

Thus, in projects with young children, we need to gain both consent
(from parents) and assent (from children). This means that children who
are capable of forming their own views should be granted the right to
express those views freely in all matters affecting them, commensurate
with their age and maturity (BERA, 2018). The process of gaining assent
is not too dissimilar from the consent sought from parents/guardians,
as 'they should be told why their participation is necessary, what they
will be asked to do, what will happen to the information they provide,
how that information will be used and how and to whom it will be
reported' (BERA, 2018: 9). This process is not always straightforward
with young children, however, especially those with special needs or
who are vulnerable. Ellis and Beauchamp (2012) assert that:

> While working with young children who have cognitive, physical,
> communicative or emotional difficulties can make the research

process more challenging, the same rights and responsibilities between the participant and the researcher should apply as those pertaining to any other research project involving children.

(p. 48)

Therefore, when explaining the project, in order to gain agreement to participate, you need to be clear 'how well the child understands what is being communicated, how able s/he is to process this information and how well s/he can express his or her own views' (Ellis and Beauchamp, 2012: 48). In addition, and more fundamental, is to consider, however much you want them to participate, whether the research should take place in the first place. In this context, Forster and Eperjesi (2017) identify that a piece of research using vulnerable subjects as participants must first weigh up the impact of the research to ensure that it carries no risk of harm.

INDIVIDUAL/GROUP TASK

Using BERA's (2018) advice, identify the steps taken to gain consent/assent in a research project that seeks the views of children, including children with special educational needs.

Overall, BERA (2018) suggests a course of action that requires researchers to take a number of steps in order to ensure clean ethical practice:

In the case of participants whose capacity, age or other vulnerable circumstance may limit the extent to which they can be expected to understand or agree voluntarily to participate, researchers should fully explore ways in which they can be supported to participate with assent in the research. In such circumstances, researchers should also seek the collaboration and approval of those responsible for such participants.

(p. 15)

Therefore, in any research project that involves young people, allowing them a voice in relation to research ethics is as significant as their importance in the research itself. As research methods become more innovative, ways of gaining assent to support informed consent and/or assent are also constantly changing. Interest in seeking young people's voices within educational research has seen a significant growth in the participation of children actively involved in research in educational settings (Bourke and Loveridge, 2014). Therefore, ethical guidance around working with young people in early education research has witnessed an equal level of growth. According to BERA (2018), 'it is normally expected that participants' voluntary consent will be obtained at the start of the study, and that researchers must remain open to the possibility that participants may want to withdraw at any time' (p. 9). Yet Solvason (2013) suggests that many view research ethics as a set of rules that they need to learn and follow in a very superficial way. However, gaining consent or implementing a code of ethics within a research project should not stop at gaining consent; clean ethical practice is in the preparation, execution and dissemination of the research – it is ongoing (Hodgkin et al., 2016).

Normally, ethical considerations will depend completely on the purpose and design of the research. It requires a reflexive approach whereby researchers engage with the issues that are raised in their own work and the context in which it takes place (Gallagher et al., 2010). In any research project that works with young people, a series of ethical issues need to be addressed early on in the process to gain informed consent. First, the ethical processes with the institutions and settings where the researcher is based will have an interest in the research, and their individual processes need to be followed. For instance, if you are a student in higher education, your university will have a specific process that needs to be followed and paperwork completed *before* research takes place. Second, you should think about whether you need to approach gatekeepers before directly approaching participants, and the specific safeguarding procedures associated with the setting (BERA, 2018). Once these issues have been addressed, the formal process of gaining written consent begins. It is important to note here that while informed consent is ongoing, it is possible to pinpoint certain stages at which it is formally organised or negotiated (Aaltonen, 2017). According to Bourke and Loveridge (2014), the process of establishing an informed consent in early childhood education often involves a three-step process: (1) the provision of adequate information; (2) checking that participants have understood what they are agreeing to; and (3) establishing how their consent or refusal to participate is to be recorded.

Examples might include an age-appropriate information sheet indicating what the project entails with an accompanying assent form in which children indicate their willingness (or not) to participate in the project. These can take many forms depending on the approach adopted within the research, but can range from colouring smiley/non-smiley faces or photographs of the child with thumbs up/thumbs down, through to more formal written forms. BERA (2018) recognises that 'since few ethical dilemmas have obvious or singular solutions, researchers will take different and creative approaches to resolving them' (p. 1), and research in early childhood education is no different.

Once assent/consent has been gained, however, it is essential that ethics remains an ongoing consideration, particularly with young children whose memory of the original consent may be short-lived. This means that they should be involved throughout the research, and ethics is more than a 'hurdle to be got out of the way at the beginning' (Hill, 2005: 65). As part of this process, when working with young children, it is important that researchers aim to continuously reflect on the power balance in the relationship. This is particularly significant in research taking place over a period of time, when time needs to be allowed at relevant regular intervals to revisit reminders about assent as young children may forget or change their minds about participation or elements of participation, or the opportunity to withdraw from the research. It is therefore paramount that when working with young children, researchers adopt a continuous responsive dynamic approach to sustained, revalidated and comfortable assent from the children.

INDIVIDUAL/GROUP TASK

How would you ensure that young children's 'voice' is considered when using video as part of ongoing consideration of ethics throughout research projects? Does it vary by the length of the project or the age of the children?

In addition to assent from the children, there are also additional consents needed from other stakeholders, including parents and settings. Parental consent is essential in protecting children from possible harm or risk in the research process, but can also present challenges, including the risk of losing willing participants. An important consideration is that 'active' consent is required, and not 'passive' consent:

which generally describe situations in which the requirement for written permission is waived unless a parent restricts their child's participation via the opt out method specified by the researcher. Under passive consent procedures, parental nonresponse is considered as a permission to participate in the research study.

(Liu et al., 2017: 46)

Passive consent could also take the form of the school attempting to give consent for the parents (e.g. by claiming that they hold 'blanket consent from parents to take part in research projects'). This would not be acceptable as parents would not have received specific details of your particular project and have not given informed consent.

The role of video and ethics

There has been consideration of the use of video in other areas of research, such as medicine (e.g. Harte et al., 2017), but much less in the field of education. One international study found this especially complicated as 'a result of diverse interpretations of international ethical codes, alongside local restrictions and ethics review processes' (Rutanen et al., 2018: 1). This study concluded that the main concern in using video data in research was 'the tension between protection of children's confidentiality and the benefits of using video scenes – as data and/ or evidence – in research' (Rutanen et al., 2018: 3). Our own experience using video suggests there are many benefits as it produces large (sometimes overwhelming) amounts of rich data, but it can be challenging to verify what we are seeing with young children, hence potentially excluding them from the research process and raising questions regarding ownership (Robson, 2011). This is further complicated by the international statutes (such as the United Nations Convention on the Rights of the Child – UNCRC) that protect the rights of chid, yet at the same time ensure their voice should be heard (White, 2017). In Wales, this is particularly important, as legal and policy frameworks are both supportive of children's rights, perhaps at odds with other areas of the UK (Tyrie and Beauchamp, 2018). In this context, research with young children using video is no different from other research with young children, which should always put the needs of the children first.

Interpreting and validating results ethically

The process of analysing and interpreting results is an ethical consideration that can influence the credibility and trustworthiness of any research project, but can also affect positively or negatively the 'voice' of the children being heard. There is therefore a need to consider ethics again when considering interpretation and validity. The underlying principle is that the data are analysed in an honest and transparent way so that the research is a 'trustworthy source of knowledge' (Ruane, 2005: 27) and, perhaps more importantly in the context of ethics, represents the views of those young children being researched. Brooks et al. (2014) contend that 'researchers always have a stake in their research and may be tempted to claim greater significance for their work than is warranted' (p. 163). It might be that data are presented to provide a more powerful set of outcomes than is needed (or reflected in the data). Applying objectivity to the analysis and interpretation of your results has always been considered good practice in ensuring that analysis is accurate and free from any researcher bias. However, as Brooks et al. (2014) also state, this might not solve the problem:

> Ethical slippage in data analysis might not always be a consciously driven behaviour. Sometimes a researcher might be overtaken by their passion for their project; sometimes a researcher may want to use their more 'sensational' findings to draw attention to a lacuna in policy and practice for the very best motives to effect social change.
>
> (pp. 163–164)

One way to deal with the potential 'ethical slippage' is to consider 'ethical reflexivity' during the research process (for more detail, see Chapter 1, this volume). This is to be aware of the researcher's own role in the in ensuring that ethical practice is clean. Brooks et al. (2014) conclude that the 'data analysis stage of research, and its ethical dimensions, deserve more explicit consideration in guidelines and training' (p. 164).

Having already established that the voice of the participants is central to the research process, in interpreting results, both from an ethical and a validation perspective, we also need to consider how this can happen. Perhaps the most important process is known as member checking, or respondent/participant validation, which is used to validate, verify or evaluate the trustworthiness and plausibility of qualitative results. It is important that this process is meaningful and not 'merely a nod to validation' (Birt et al., 2016: 1802). It can be a single event or take place at key points in the research process. In traditional research, such as interviews with adults, this may take the form of giving interviewees a transcript of the interview and checking for accuracy, and later returning to present findings to them to see if this accords with what they thought they were saying. In essence, the researcher is both triangulating and validating their interpretation within the research team and, more importantly, with those being researched. As such, the aim is to encourage 'negotiation of meaning' between the participant and the researcher (Doyle, 2007). In more innovative research methods, the process is less straightforward, and becomes particularly complicated with young children or those with communication or cognitive challenges. This does not mean, however, that member checking is any less important with these groups; it just presents the research team with different challenges to find an appropriate method or approach to use.

Sharing and dissemination of research findings in a variety of forms

The role of ethics within any research project starts in the planning stage of the project, continues through data collection and analysis, but importantly continues through to the dissemination of the research. It is important to note here that the 'right to withdraw' also continues throughout the project and requires consideration on the part of the researcher up until this point, and explicit permission for dissemination in all forms is essential. A particular concern when using video is that video (like photographs) provides an identifiable image of the child, even if anonymised, including using still images from the video. In addition, the actual voice of the child is recorded and may also be identifiable in any dissemination. This means that a certain level of technical skill is needed by the researcher or support from elsewhere is needed to anonymise video data. This can take many forms, but in a study of medical practitioners' views of different methods of anonymising video of surgery for training purposes, where similar issues arise, it was found that:

Not surprisingly, the greater the alteration of the video, the more it was perceived as anonymous. Yet there is a delicate balance between processing adequately for anonymity and overprocessing to the point of unsuitability for research purposes. We believe that facial blurring achieves this balance for most applications.

(Silas et al., 2015: 275)

In addition to anonymity, in disseminating research, there is a significant ethical duty to the children involved, as 'data should speak for themselves. Your analysis should reveal the message behind the data, and not be used to select only the results that are convenient to you' (Walliman and Buckler, 2008: 41). A potential ethical dilemma is that a researcher can be caught up in the tension of needing to report their findings accurately while preventing harm and respecting their participants (Henderson, 2008). Inevitably, in social science research, an element of critique or evaluation is involved when disseminating the research. This can (as alluded to earlier) add to the tension surrounding sharing and disseminating the research in a clean and ethical manner. Brooks et al. (2014) suggest useful advice on this issue: 'The bottom line is that researchers aim for what the call "accuracy, credibility or trustworthiness" in how they present their findings – and this is not often a straightforward process. It is bedevilled with ethical concerns' (p. 165).

INDIVIDUAL/GROUP TASK

You have completed your early childhood research project. The manager of the setting would like to read through the findings once you have completed your analysis. How does this impact upon the presentation of your findings? What do you need to consider as part of this process?

Summary

This chapter has explored how ethical concerns can be addressed in early childhood education research. This included a variety of visual and technological solutions, a consideration of informed consent/assent, appropriate means of gaining each from young children, particularly with children with special educational needs, interpreting and validating results, and the sharing and dissemination of research findings in a variety of forms:

- Research ethics in early childhood education must be seen as an ongoing process.

- As research methods become more innovative (e.g. the use of video within research), a greater emphasis must be placed on the need for clean and participative ethical practice.

- In any project that works closely with young people, the need to listen to their 'voice' on an ongoing basis throughout the research process is essential for truly ethical practice.

Recommended reading

Alderson, P., and Morrow, V. (2011) *The Ethics of Research with Children and Young People: A Practical Handbook*. London: Sage.

Bourke, R. and Loveridge, J. (2014) Exploring informed consent and dissent through children's participation in educational research. *International Journal of Research and Method in Education*, 37(2): 151–165.

British Education Research Association (BERA) (2018) *Ethical Guidelines for Educational Research*. London: BERA.

Solvason, C. (2013) Research and the early years practitioner researcher. *Early Years*, 33(1): 90–97.

White, E. (2017) Video ethics and young children. *Video Journal of Education and Pedagogy*, 2(1): 1–2.

References

Aaltonen, S. (2017) Challenges in gaining and re-gaining informed consent among young people on the margins of education. *International Journal of Social Research Methodology*, 20(4): 329–341.

Alderson, P., and Morrow, V. (2011) *The Ethics of Research with Children and Young People: A Practical Handbook*. London: Sage.

Birt, L., Scott, S., Cavers, D., Campbell, C. and Walter, F. (2016) Member checking: a tool to enhance trustworthiness or merely a nod to validation? *Qualitative Health Research*, 26(13): 1802–1811.

Bourke, R. and Loveridge, J. (2014) Exploring informed consent and dissent through children's participation in educational research. *International Journal of Research and Method in Education*, 37(2): 151–165.

British Education Research Association (BERA) (2018) *Ethical Guidelines for Educational Research*. London: BERA.

Brooks, R., Riele, K. and Maguire, M. (2014) *Ethics and Education Research*. London: Sage.

Coyne, I. (2010) Research with children and young people: the issue of parental (proxy) consent. *Children & Society*, 24(3): 227–237.

Doyle, S. (2007) Member checking with older women: a framework for negotiating meaning. *Health Care for Women International*, 28(10): 888–908.

Ellis, C. and Beauchamp, G. (2012) Ethics in working with and researching children with special educational needs. In I. Palaiologou (ed.), *Ethical Practice in Early Children*. London: Sage, pp. 47–60.

Forster, C. and Eperjesi, R. (2017) *Action Research for New Teachers: Evidence-Based Evaluation of Practice*. London: Sage.

Gallagher, M., Haywood, S., Jones, M.W. and Milne, S. (2010) Negotiating informed consent with children in school-based research: a critical review. *Children & Society*, 24(6): 471–482.

Green D. (2012) Involving young children in research. In I. Palaiologou (ed.), *Ethical Practice in Early Children*. London: Sage, pp. 15–31.

Harte, J., Homer, C., Sheehan, A., Leap, N. and Foureur, M. (2017) Using video in childbirth research: ethical approval challenges. *Nursing Ethics*, 24(2): 177–189.

Henderson, R. (2008) Dangerous terrains: negotiating ethical dilemmas. In R. Henderson and P. Danaher (eds), *Troubling Terrains: Tactics for Traversing and Transforming Contemporary Educational Research*. Queensland: Post Pressed, pp. 211–222.

Hill, M. (2005) Ethical considerations in researching children's experiences. In S. Green and D. Hogan (eds), *Researching Children's Experience: Methods and Approaches*. London: Sage, pp. 61–86.

Hodgkin, K., Fleming, S., Beauchamp, G. and Bryant, A. (2016) 'We thought you were undercover, here to inspect us': some of the challenges of ethnographic fieldwork in schools. *Wales Journal of Education*, 18(2): 105–109.

Israel, M. and Hay, I. (2006) *Research Ethics for Social Scientists*. London: Sage.

Liu, C., Cox, R.B., Washburn, I.J., Croff, J.M. and Crethar, H.C. (2017) The effects of requiring parental consent for research on adolescents' risk behaviors: a meta-analysis'. *Journal of Adolescent Health*, 61(1): 45–52.

Miller, T. and Boulton, M. (2007) Changing constructions of informed consent: Qualitative research and complex social worlds. *Social Science & Medicine*, 65: 2199–2211.

Robson, S. (2011). Producing and using video data in the early years: ethical questions and practical consequences in research with young children. *Children & Society*, 25(3): 179–189.

Ruane, J.M. (2005) *Essentials of Research Methods: A Guide to Social Science Research*. Hoboken, NJ: Blackwell.

Rutanen, N., Amorim, K., Marwick, D. and White, H. (2018) Tensions and challenges concerning ethics on video research with young children: experiences from an international collaboration among seven countries. *Video Journal of Education and Pedagogy*, 3(1): 1–14.

Silas, M.R., Grassia, P. and Langerman, A. (2015) Video recording of the operating room: is anonymity possible? *Journal of Surgical Research*, 197(2): 272–276.

Solvason, C. (2013) Research and the early years practitioner researcher. *Early Years*, 33(1): 90–97.

Tyrie, J. and Beauchamp, G. (2018) Children's perceptions of their access to rights in Wales: the relevance of gender and age. *International Journal of Children's Rights*, 26: 1–27.

Walliman, N. and Buckler, S. (2008) *Your Dissertation in Education*. London: Sage.

White, E. (2017) Video ethics and young children. *Video Journal of Education and Pedagogy*, 2(1): 1–2.

Going beyond participatory ideology when doing research with young children

The case for ethical permeability and relatability

Ioanna Palaiologou

Introduction

Participatory ideology in research with young children has seen increased interest recently, with many researchers seeking to understand both the enactment of children's rights and ways of empowering young children in the research process (e.g. Alderson and Morrow, 2011; Christensen and James, 2008; Clark, 2003; Clark and Moss, 2001; Clark et al., 2005, 2014; Dahlberg and Moss, 2005; Edminston, 2008; Gallacher and Gallagher, 2008; Harcourt et al., 2011; Hart, 1992; Murray, 2016, 2017; Palaiologou, 2014a; Powell et al., 2016; Punch, 2002; Sargeant and Harcourt, 2012; Shier, 2001; Waller and Bitou, 2011). The quest for participatory research is based on the notion of an agentic child who is offered 'space' to be heard for his or her views and will have these respected and acted upon. Participatory early childhood researchers associate participation with voice(s) and an increasing emphasis on listening to children's various languages (e.g. Clark and Moss, 2005; Ingold, 2011; Prout, 2011; Moss and Petrie, 2002; Thomson, 2011), and critically pressing for greater participation by children, recognition of voice(s) and agency to enact this in research and practice.

As shown in this book, researchers have started to seek laudable and creative ways to engage children in research as equals or at least to ensure that children have their own epistemological understandings on how knowledge is constructed. Academic research in early childhood and practice has seen the flourishing of several methods such as the mosaic approach, as well as art-based and visual methods where children are becoming researchers of their own lives. These are detailed in chapters in this book. For instance, Biffi and Zuccoli in Chapter 4 detail arts as a research method, and Kingdon in Chapter 8 explores the use of the mosaic approach as an ethnographic methodology. However, some (e.g. Alderson, 2012; Hammersley, 2015) have raised questions on the practicality of children's participation in research, especially when it comes to very young children (e.g. Elwick and Sumsion, 2013; Elwick et al., 2014a, 2014b; Sumsion, 2014).

Thus, based on findings from two research projects (Palaiologou, 2014a, 2017a) and other previous work (Palaiologou, 2012, 2014b, 2017b, in press; Salamon and Palaiologou, in press), the term participation is discussed to explore some challenges it presents. Without dismissing the quest for enacting children's voice(s) and agency, I will argue that attention should be paid to ethics as an expanded notion of participation. Finally, I propose that our thinking on research should go beyond how to ensure participation, and instead see ethical praxis as central to such research, making the case for ethical permeability and relatability as parameters for participatory research. I will conclude that research with young children should be reconceptualised as a hybrid between participation and ethical praxis.

INDIVIDUAL/GROUP TASK

Before you read this chapter, consider what participation means to you. What do you think participatory research is?

My story so far

Although the arguments here build upon two research projects and its findings, my thinking in conceptualising research with young children and critically problematising participation is still shaping and developing.

The first project explored in this chapter examined how researchers can achieve participation of young children in research and what methods are enabling young children to become co-researchers (Palaiologou, 2014b). It employed content analysis of 150 research papers in peer-reviewed journals from 2012 to 2014 and interviews with 12 active researchers. The key findings from the analysis showed:

- most of the research refers to children above the age of 4 years old;

- very little/limited research with children under 4 years old;

- participation becomes more problematic when it comes to working with very young children;

- access issues on researching the voices of very young children;

- a phobia to certain research methods (i.e. focusing on interpretative approaches as the only participatory method);

- lack of integral conversations between adults to admit weaknesses in their position and possible mistakes;

- limited discussion of the concept that is central to empowerment/ participation of children;

- a focus on creation of 'spaces' that tend to be adult-oriented, rather than the provision of a conversational context in which the relationship is permeable in terms of 'adult power' over the children; and

- asymmetrical relationships between research and children in terms of empowering both parties.

It was concluded that the debate of participatory research is fragmented and tends to focus only on discourses of the mechanism (methods) of participation (how to do participation), rather than trying to explore the whole story (theoretical conceptualisation) and its axiological elements.

The second project (Palaiologou, 2017a) was a meta-analysis of ethical codes of established association and analysis of the dominant participatory models. These are as follows:

1. Hart, R. (1992) *Children's Participation: From Tokenism to Citizenship.* Florence: UNICEF International Child Development Centre.
2. Shier, H. (2001) Pathways to participation: openings, opportunities and obligations. *Children & Society*, 15(2): 107–117.
3. Kirby, P., Lanyon, C., Cronin, K. and Sinclair, R. (2003) *Building a Culture of Participation: Involving Children and Young People in Policy, Service Planning, Delivery and Evaluation.* London: Department for Education and Skills.

It was found that:

■   ethical codes and the models of participation are adult-oriented and there is limited control or even participation on ethical codes and models;

■   there was limited discussion of an axiomatic understanding of what is required for conducting ethically sound research with, for, by and about young children; and

■   participatory research should publicly debate ethical anxieties and dilemmas, and *not* be haunted by them.

It concluded that participatory research should add another dimension: *permeability*, first as a way of evaluating research and to what extent the outcomes will alter the 'spaces' of children; and second, the extent and ways that the research will be transmitted through the participants.

Both projects have allowed me to start developing my conceptualisation around participatory ideology that is presented in the following sections.

The paradoxes of young children's participation

The notion of children's participation as a fundamental right emerged from the introduction of the UNCRC (1989), paired with a new wave in the study of childhood that promoted and advocated children's agency and voice(s). Aspiring to principles of participation that allowed space and place for children's voice(s) and agency in an adult-oriented world, academic research focused on examining how the agentic nature of young children can be expressed at all levels of their lives. The literature referenced throughout this chapter has seen a new wave of research where, as mantra for voice and agency, children are invited to be participants within their own terms (child-led research).

The notion of participation is understood as 'manifestation of individual agency within a social context' (Percy-Smith and Thomas, 2010: 357), a dialogical and democratic relationship where all are active participants, share power and have control in decision-making by being co-researchers or co-producers of knowledge (Phillips, 2011). 'The essence of participation is exercising voice and choice and developing the human, organisational and management capacity to solve problems as they arise in order to sustain improvement' (Saxena, 2011: 31). In earlier literature on childhood studies, such as Hart's (1992) ladder of participation or Shier's (2001) pathways to participation, models were offered to guide us, identifying steps in children's participation as reflective points. These models have become increasingly criticised as adult-oriented and limiting choice about what to share with children (Gallacher and Gallagher, 2008; Head, 2011). Meanwhile, other research (Alderson, 2010) urges us to reconceptualise participation and seek either for broader definitions when children are considered, or acknowledge the centrality of the participatory language with terms such as dialogue, power, shared experiences, mutuality and collective action(s).

In early childhood research, the language of participation is now commonly used in economically wealthy countries, with evidence of several changes in research impacting on practice to where children appear to be leading the research (e.g. Waller and Bitou, 2011). However, a body of literature has also emerged that examines young children's participation, voice(s) and agency, which recognises the limitations, paradoxes and tensions of children's participation and empowerment (Hammersley, 2015; I'Anson, 2013; Thomson, 2011). For example, one of the key tensions is evolving around children's rights, which focuses on four key areas: survival, developmental, protection and participatory rights. However, the protection or promotion of participatory rights might bring an imbalance that can lead to tensions in implementing the other rights. Philo (2011), for example, illustrates a tension between protection and participation rights in life situations and, in examining children's voices in life situations, cautions us that there are occasions where this cannot always be possible or appropriate. He offers the example of a situation where listening to children's voices can be inappropriate, as in the case where a child expresses the wish to form a sexual relationship with an adult. Instead, he proposes that:

> There are moments when it is imperative [not to be] 'seduced' by children's own voices, but instead retaining a (thoroughly and reflexively critical) sense of the adult discourses [. . .] which cannot but 'see further and deeper' than is ever possible for the children themselves.
>
> (Philo, 2011: 125)

In line with the UNCRC (1989), adults need to safeguard children's survival, developmental and protection rights. In doing so, there are occasions where protection rights become more imperative, as, for instance, if a child is ill and not allowed for medical reasons to eat a certain food, the adult is responsible to make sure that the child is not eating it. Similarly, many children do not enjoy injections, but as adults we have to make sure they are vaccinated. Thus, there are certain occasions when, as adults, we have to ignore children's wishes as we try to protect them so their survival rights are not threatened.

In research with young children, and especially with under threes, these tensions equally become barriers for participation, and searching for research that will engage children as equal partners does not come without its challenges. To begin, research as a process, with its philosophy, mechanisms, forms of articulation and dissemination strategies, is adult-constructed and involves representational codes (writing, analysis) and practices (data collection) that are meaningful and understood by adults. Consequently, for a research project to claim that it is participatory, it is vital that these codes are meaningful and understood by both children and adults. Yet children, and especially very young ones, are still developing physically, emotionally, socially and cognitively, so it is argued that we cannot ignore their developmental nature as this has impact on how their voices are expressed and represented, and the level of their involvement in participatory research. As Lee and Motzkau (2011), using infancy as an example, reflect on this:

> The multiplicity of 'voice' centrally concerns the ethico-political matter of children's representation and participation [. . .]. But it

also concerns maturation as a passage from voice but speechless infancy [. . .] and the complex interplay this has with many circumstances in which children can and cannot find voice, along with the range of institutional and technological conditions in which their voices are interpreted, mediated and amplified.

(p. 11)

Moreover, operationalising young children's participations has further paradoxes, as there are contested arenas of decision-making about who is in control of the design of the research project (i.e. methodology), the choice of theoretical conceptualisation (i.e. axiology, ontology, epistemology) and how the constructed knowledge is disseminated (i.e. choice of articulating the research findings) for which formidable barriers are posed by the developmental nature of young children (Palaiologou, 2014a, 2016, in press). Consequently, some researchers, in their quest for children's voice(s) to be heard, have solicited efforts to examine participatory mechanisms (mainly methods), and this has led to attempts examining how (methods) and by what (topics that can be understood by children) we *do* participation. Yet participation means that all take part and are in control of decision-making at all stages in the form of a dialogue between different parties (adults and children). In participatory research, this poses critical questions as to what the degree of influence and control of children is in the overall research process (at axiological, ontological, epistemological and methodological levels), how children as partners in research are positioned in relation to themselves (epistemological stance) and to the adults, and how the issue of power is recognised and framed.

Finally, participation requires responsibility and accountability from all parties involved. Both concepts are instrumental elements of voice(s) and agency, and hence the challenge ahead lies in recognising that by enlisting them as participants in research, we might ask them too much too soon. Also, as adults, instead of liberating children's agentic nature when they are invited to participatory research, we might achieve the reverse by not respecting their right to be children. With this in mind, the quest for children's participation means more than merely taking part in research. By empowering them to make and shape their own lives and spaces for participation purposes, this places high levels of accountability and responsibility on young children who, developmentally, might not be able to respond. Research affects people's lives, and, in that sense, when asking very young children to influence either their own lives or those of others, this may be problematic when they are still trying to make sense of their own identity and place in the social world.

Literature on participatory research is valuable and has offered us a shift from adult-oriented/-imposed limits on how children's lives are seen to accept that children's voice(s) and agency are vital for research and practice, as well as stressing the importance of reciprocal relationships between children and adults. When it comes to very young children, however, the focus has been on participatory mechanisms (methods and practice), with limited attempts to reconstruct what participation means. This runs the risk of reducing the concept of participation from the right to exercise agency to mechanisms and strategies on how to *do* participation. Again, while research that explores how to *do* participation is valuable, in previous work I have argued that when it comes to very young children, especially the ones under the age of 3, participation is an illusion as there are tensions at axiomatical and ontological levels (Palaiologou, 2014a, 2017b, in press; Salamon and Palaiologou, in press). I have concluded, for example, that 'participatory research with young children should move beyond mere participation and into a critical engagement on ethical research as ethics should be the fundamental key notion of research with young children' (Palaiologou, 2014a: 692).

In early childhood, we should seek therefore to go further, deeper and *beyond* in our thinking on participatory research and note that participation with very young children cannot be truly achieved. Instead, we should move beyond and acknowledge partnerships with children in research where the empowerment element is the ethical orientation of this research: ethical praxis and its permeability and relatability, as will be explained below.

INDIVIDUAL/GROUP TASK

Can you identify any other tensions in participatory research with children? What are the challenges when researching the lives of infants and toddlers? Can you achieve participatory research?

Beyond participation: ethical praxis

The notion of praxis is rooted in classical philosophy. The term refers to actions in which humans are engaged, and can be described as:

> a form of socially established cooperative human activity that involves characteristics forms understanding (sayings), modes of action (doings) and the ways in which people relate to one another and the world (relatings).
>
> (Kemmis et al., 2014: 155)

The notion of praxis is not limited only to actions, but actions based on reflection where one 'makes a wise and prudent practical judgement about how to act in *this* situation' (Carr and Kemmis, 1986: 190, original emphasis). These judgements on how to act are based on good decisions (eupraxia) or bad ones (dyspraxia).

As mentioned earlier, in early childhood we should reconceptualise participation based on 'forms of understanding' that relate to children by respecting the continual interplay between their developmental and agentic nature. Instead of being hounded on how to do participation with very young children, therefore, I have argued that the concern should be eupraxia, 'where the causality between adult actions and children's actions is the locus of consideration' (Palaiologou 2014a: 696). I argue that rather than striving for generalisations that homogenise participatory research with children, it might be better to move the discourse towards more heterogeneity where we explore ethical praxis with children and seek for potentialities that are respectful of their rights. Achieving ethical praxis in research with young children can be embodied in participation, as to have agency within a social context, as suggested by Percy-Smith and Thomas (2010), an imperative condition is the creation of an ethical terrain of research based on context and situational actions: permeability (i.e. emotional responsiveness to children) and relatability (i.e. emotional relatability to children and children's spaces) (Salamon and Palaiologou, in press).

INDIVIDUAL/GROUP TASK

What do you think the role of ethics is in research?

The case for ethical permeability and relatability

Within the current literature, the act of participation involves agency, voice(s), awareness of the other, respect and reciprocity, advocacy, dialogicality, and shared responsibility. However, it is suggested here that in early childhood research, we need to reconceptualise our thinking and re-examine participation through the lenses of ethical permeability and relatability.

Permeability and relatability as parameters allow us to acknowledge emotional responses in research. First, permeability helps us to see whether young children are in distress or feel uncomfortable in a situation where adults' actions affect their behaviour, where relatability offers the power for an adult to stop a research situation. Second, researchers can control the creation and process of research situations by ethically establishing actions that are permeable, responsive and relatable to children, rather than actions for which both parties are responsible and accountable.

Finally, the issue of power in research has been the concern of many researchers in participatory research with children, with adults always having the power, and thus being unequal to children. Permeability as a parameter will allow the adult to get a sense of his or her power (e.g. physical size, language that is used), however, and relate to the child's world, rather than try to understand it and become equal to the child. In that sense, the imbalance of power between children and adult becomes permissible, instead of being limited (which is impossible), so long as ethical actions have been considered (for further details on ethical considerations in early childhood education, see Chapter 2, this volume).

In this chapter, I have not suggested that discussion on ethical praxis, adding permeability and relatability as key parameters, is yet complete. What is suggested, however, is that we do need to rethink participatory research with young children and move our thinking beyond the mechanisms (how to do participation) and frame it as ethical praxis. As parameters of participation, ethical permeability and relatability offer alternative ways of thinking that, although challenging, provide opportunities to understand the multiplicities of research with children.

Conclusion: the hybrids of research with young children

Prout (2005) argued that 'the social view of childhood is counterposed to a natural of biological one', and the view of the 'children as social actors' is now shadowing and ignoring the biological/developmental child (p. 2). He proposed that instead of only favouring the view of the child as social actor:

> Childhood studies [should] move beyond the opposition of nature and culture [. . . to] a hybrid form [. . . wherein] children's capacities are extended and supplemented by all kinds of material artefacts and technologies, which are also hybrids of nature and culture.
>
> (Prout, 2005: 3–4)

Building on this idea, I argue that research with children should be a hybrid at two ideological levels: constructs of childhood and constructs of participation.

First, as shown above, research with very young children cannot merely be participatory or seen only as agentic. The dichotomy of the agentic versus the developmental child is not helping to move *beyond* in research with children. Research with young children should acknowledge both aspects of children's nature and accommodate them as important and complementary, rather than competing, and seek ways to make them part of reflexive critical thinking on how we conduct research with children.

Second, I am suggesting that participation and ethical praxis should become a hybrid so that ethics and participation in research stand next to each other. Ethics tends normally to be considered as a process that allows participatory research to take place. Here, it is proposed that participation and ethics should be entangled in research, and, instead of being concerned with participatory research, should go beyond and allow hybrid research with young children as a potentiality to diverse children's voice(s) and agency, as well acknowledging their developmental nature.

Summary

■ A different way of thinking about children in research has emerged in the current century, leading to a methodological shift 'from being unknowing *objects* of research to aware *subjects*, and [. . .] active participants' (Powell et al., 2016: 197, original emphasis).

■ This is now commonly promoted within an ideology where children have the right to be properly researched.

■ Attention has been paid on how and in what ways researchers can empower children in the quest for participatory 'child-friendly' methods designed to be relevant, applicable and to eliminate voicelessness in research (Cahill, 2004).

■ Children are now viewed as active participants 'on the basis of who they are, rather than who they will become' (Moss and Petrie, 2002: 6).

■ However, 'participatory methods are no less problematic, or ethically ambiguous, than any other methods' (Gallacher and Gallagher, 2008: 513).

■ 'The fundamental questions on how we can achieve *participatory research* with young children should be moderated to how we can achieve *ethical research* with young children where children are encouraged to take responsibility and ownership, while at the same time autonomy and shared responsibility is encouraged [. . .] as ethics should be the fundamental key notion of research with young children' (Palaiologou, 2014a: 692, original emphasis).

■ Participatory research should add two dimensions – permeability and relatability – as a way of evaluating research and to what extent the outcomes will alter the 'spaces' of children.

Recommended reading

This book discusses the constructions of childhood:

Prout, A. (2005) *The Future of Childhood*. London: Routledge.

The following articles are critical examinations of participation and children's rights:

Percy-Smith, B. (2010) Councils, consultation and community: rethinking the spaces for children and young people's participation. *Children's Geographies*, 8: 107–122.

Powell, M.A., Graham, A. and Truscott, J. (2016) Ethical research involving children: facilitating reflexive engagement. *Qualitative Research Journal*, 16(2): 197–208.

Punch, S. (2002) Research with children: the same or different from research with adults? *Childhood*, 9(3): 321–341.

References

Alderson, P. (2010) Younger children's individual participation in all matters affecting the child. In N. Thomas and B. Perry Smith (eds), *A Handbook of Children's Rights and Young People's Participation: Perspectives from Theory to Practice*. London: Routledge, pp. 88–89.

Alderson, P. (2012) Rights-respecting research: a commentary on 'The right to be properly researched: research with children in a messy, real world'. *Children's Geographies*, 7(4): 233–239.

Alderson, P. and Morrow, V. (2011) *The Ethics of Research with Children and People: A Practical Handbook*, 2nd edn. London: Sage.

Cahill, C. (2004) Defying gravity? Raising consciousness through collective research. *Children's Geographies*, 2(2): 273–286.

Carr, W. and Kemmis, S. (1986) *Becoming Critical: Education, Knowledge and Action Research*. Lewes: Falmer Press.

Christensen, P. and James, A. (2008) *Research with Children: Perspectives and Practices*, 2nd edn. London: Routledge.

Clark, A. (2003) The mosaic approach and research with young children. In V. Lewis, M. Kellett, C. Robinson, S. Fraser and S. Ding (eds), *The Reality of Research with Children and Young People*. London: Sage, pp. 142–161.

Clark, A. and Moss, P. (2001) *Listening to Young Children: The Mosaic Approach*. London: Joseph Rowntree Foundation.

Clark, A. and Moss, P. (2005) *Spaces to Play: More Listening to Young Children Using the Mosaic Approach*. London: National Children's Bureau.

Clark, A., Kjørholt, A.T. and Moss, P. (eds) (2005) *Beyond Listening to Children on Early Childhood Services*. Bristol: Policy Press.

Clark, A., Flewitt, R., Hammersley, M. and Rob, M. (eds) (2014) *Understanding Research with Children and Young People*. London: Sage.

Dahlberg, G. and Moss, P. (2005) *Ethics and Politics in Early Childhood Education*. London: RoutledgeFalmer.

Edminston, B. (2008) *Forming Ethical Identities in Early Childhood Play*. London: Routledge.

Elwick, S. and Sumsion, J. (2013) Moving beyond utilitarian perspectives of infant participation in participatory research: film-mediated research encounters. *International Journal of Early Years Education*, 21(4): 336–347.

Elwick, S., Bradley, B. and Sumsion, J. (2014a) Infants as Other: uncertainties, difficulties and (im)possibilities in researching infants' lives. *International Journal of Qualitative Studies in Education*, 27(2): 196–213.

Elwick, S., Bradley, B. and Sumsion, J. (2014b) Creating space for infants to influence ECEC practice: the encounter, écart, reversibility and ethical reflection. *Educational Philosophy and Theory*, 46(8): 873–885.

Gallacher, L. and Gallagher, G. (2008) Methodological immaturity in childhood research? Thinking through 'participatory methods'. *Childhood*, 15(4): 499–516.

Hammersley, M. (2015) Research ethics and the concept of children's rights. *Children & Society*, 29: 569–582.

Harcourt, D., Perry, B. and Waller, T. (eds) (2011) *Researching Young Children's Perspectives*. London: Routledge.

Hart, R. (1992) *Children's Participation: From Tokenism to Citizenship*. Florence: UNICEF International Child Development Centre.

Head, B. (2011) Why not ask them? Mapping and prompting youth participation. *Children and Youth Services Review*, 22: 541–547.

I'Anson, J. (2013) Beyond the child's voice: towards an ethics for children's participation rights. *Global Studies of Education*, 3(1): 104–114.

Ingold, T. (2011) *Being Alive: Essays on Movement, Knowledge and Description*. London: Routledge.

Kemmis, S., Heikkinen, H.L., Fransson, G., Aspfors, J. and Edwards-Groves, C. (2014) Mentoring of new teachers as a contested practice: supervision, support and collaborative self-development. *Teaching and Teacher Education*, 43: 154–164.

Kirby, P., Lanyon, C., Cronin, K. and Sinclair, R. (2003) *Building a Culture of Participation: Involving Children and Young People in Policy, Service Planning, Delivery and Evaluation*. London: Department for Education and Skills.

Lee, N. and Motzkau, J. (2011) Navigating the biopolitics of childhood. *Childhood*, 18: 7–19.

Moss, P. and Petrie, P. (2002) *From Children's Services to Children's Spaces*. London: Routledge.

Murray, J. (2016) Young children as researchers: children aged four to eight years engage in important research behaviour when they base decisions on evidence. *European Early Childhood Education Research Journal*, 24(5): 705–720.

Murray, J. (2017) Welcome in! How the academy can warrant recognition of young children as researchers. *European Early Childhood Education Research Journal*, 25(2): 224–242.

Palaiologou, I. (ed.) (2012) *Ethical Practice in Early Childhood*. London: Sage.

Palaiologou, I. (2014a) 'Do we hear what children want to say?' Ethical praxis when choosing research tools with children under five. *Early Child Development and Care*, 184(5): 689–705.

Palaiologou, I. (2014b) *The Axiological Challenges in Participatory Research with Young Children: Fragmentation or Empowerment?* Paper presented at the 24th European Early Childhood Education Research Association Conference, 7–10 September 2014, Crete, Greece.

Palaiologou, I. (2016) Ethical issues associated with educational research. In I. Palaiologou, D. Needham and T. Male (eds), *Doing Research in Education: Theory and Practice*. London: Sage, pp. 37–58.

Palaiologou, I. (2017a) *Moving Beyond Participatory Ideology When Doing Research with Young Children: The Case for Ethical Permeability*. Paper presented at ECER 2017, 'Reforming Education and the Imperative of Constant Change: Ambivalent Roles of Policy and Educational Research', 21–25 August 2017, Copenhagen, Denmark.

Palaiologou, I., (2017b) The use of vignettes in participatory research with young children. *International Journal of Early Years Education*, 15(3): 308–332.

Palaiologou, I. (in press) 'Otherness' in research with infants: marginality or potentiality? In J. Murrary, B. Swandener and K. Smith (eds), *Routledge Handbook on the Rights of the Child*. London: Routledge.

Percy-Smith, B. and Thomas, N. (2010) Conclusions: emerging themes and new directions. In N. Thomas and B. Percy-Smith (eds), *A Handbook of Children's Rights and Young People's Participation: Perspectives from Theory to Practice*. London: Routledge, pp. 356–366.

Phillips, L. (2011) *The Promise of Dialogue: The Dialogic Turn in the Production and Communication of Knowledge*. Amsterdam: John Benjamins.

Philo, C. (2011) Foucault, sexuality and when not to listen to children. *Children's Geographies*, 9: 123–127.

Powell, M.A., Graham, A. and Truscott, J. (2016) Ethical research involving children: facilitating reflexive engagement. *Qualitative Research*, 16(2): 197–208.

Prout, A. (2005) *The Future of Childhood*. London: Routledge.

Prout, A. (2011) Taking a step away from modernity: reconsidering the new sociology of childhood. *Global Studies of Childhood*, 1(1): 4–14.

Punch, S. (2002) Research with children: the same or different from research with adults? *Childhood*, 9(3): 321–341.

Salamon, A. and Palaiologou, I. (in press) Infants' and toddlers' rights in early childhood settings: research perspectives informing pedagogical practice. In F. Press and S. Cheeseman (eds), *(Re)conceptualising Children's Rights in Infant-Toddler Early Childhood Care and Education: Transnational Conversations*. Victoria: Springer.

Sargeant, J. and Harcourt, D. (2012) *Doing Ethical Research with Children*. Maidenhead: Open University Press.

Saxena, N.C. (2011) What is meant by people's participation? In A. Cornwall (ed.), *The Participation Reader*. London: Zed Books, pp. 31–33.

Shier, H. (2001) Pathways to participation: openings, opportunities and obligations. *Children & Society*, 15(2): 107–117.

Sumsion, J. (2014) Opening up possibilities through team research: an investigation of infants' lives in early childhood education. *Qualitative Research*, 14(2): 149–165.

Thomson, P. (2011) Coming to terms with 'voice'. In G. Czerniawski and W. Kidd (eds), *The International Handbook of Student Voice*. Bingley: Emerald, pp. 19–30.

Waller, T. and Bitou, A. (2011) Research with children: three challenges for participatory research in early childhood. *European Early Childhood Education Research Journal*, 19(1): 5–20.

PART II
Researching with children

4 Art as a method of research

Elisabetta Biffi and Franca Zuccoli

Introduction

The fact that art, images, drawing, and the use of expressive materials feature strongly in the lives of young children scarcely requires confirmation, yet it is borne out by numerous studies (Boone, 2008; Twigg and Garvis, 2010; Wright, 2012) and the everyday observations of early childhood education practitioners. Nevertheless, realising the full potential of the artistic dimension – which is so specific to human development – is quite a different matter. In this chapter, we explore the value of the artistic and expressive medium for children and adults in research, first in general, then as a resource for enhancing communication and relationships, and finally as a domain of inquiry and discovery that can span a diverse range of disciplinary areas.

We also examine art as a mode of research, in terms of art-based research and art-informed research paradigms (Knowles and Cole, 2008), and specifically in relation to educational contexts. Shifting from a model of everyday educational practice in which children's drawings and artistic-expressive productions are a recurrent feature but seen as offering few insights from a research perspective, to a model of inquiry that uses art as a medium through which to document, reflect, and conduct research, represents a crucial new departure that, however, is not yet perceived as a priority.

INDIVIDUAL/GROUP TASK

Before you read this chapter, consider how you would define the role of the arts in early childhood education. How would you define art-based inquiry?

Reflections on art and children: art in early childhood education

Educationalists, as well as artists, educators and teachers, have debated the role of art education both in early childhood education settings and at all subsequent levels of schooling. The most frequently recurring question is whether art may be taught or not, an issue that derives from a broader and even longer-standing discussion among philosophers, aesthetes and artists concerning the definability of art. Without attempting to engage in depth with this difficult question, we formulate some positions here that are also salient to our subsequent treatment of art as a mode of inquiry, especially in the humanities. The first of these propositions is informed by the thinking of philosopher and art critic Dino Formaggio (1973), who said that 'Art is all that men call Art' (p. 9). At first glance, this definition appears to be a mere tautology. In reality, however, it releases us from the obligation to classify art, brings back into question the criteria applied during the various historic periods, and situates the work of art in its concrete realisation. With regard to the possibility of art education, scholars have expressed a range of strongly divergent views: from those who advocate direct artistic experience for children, such as John Dewey (1995), to those who design art activities to be carried out in a context of play (Munari, 2004), and from those who see art as a vehicle for education across a range of disciplines, as proposed by Herbert Read (1958), to those who, like Arno Stern (1966), conceptualise an individual activity that does not necessarily need to be shared with others, draws on individual unconscious memory, demands a dedicated time and space, and follows a developmental trajectory.

The words of John Dewey (1995) suggest that art bears immense potential to reveal hidden meanings, other than those that are already known and shared:

Through art, meanings of objects that are otherwise dumb, incho-
ate, restricted and resisted are clarified and concentrated, and not
by thought working laboriously upon them, nor by escape into a
world of mere sense, but by creation of a new experience.

(p. 154)

Elsewhere in Dewey's seminal text *Art as Experience*, as well as in a
vast body of articles devoted to this theme, we find further references
to the power of art to fulfil exploratory, cognitive, communicative and
social functions, provided that we take it as direct experience to be
engaged with (in Dewey's view, this principle holds true for both children and adults), so he writes:

Art [. . .] intercepts every shade of expressiveness found in objects
and orders them in a new experience of life. Because objects of art
are expressive, they communicate. I do not say that communication to others is the intent of the artist. But it is the consequence
of his work – which indeed lives only in communication when it
operates in the experience of others.

(Dewey, 1995: 121–122)

The characteristics of art that we have briefly outlined must be borne in
mind, both when engaging children in art activities and when conducting art-based research; in sum, it is especially important that art should
remain active, consumable and experimental. This is the value that
springs from artistic experience, which is aesthetic experience involving
the perception and enjoyment of beauty, but above all active experience
engaging the person in practical action and reflection. Dewey argued
that the formative power of art lies precisely in this experiential dimension, with its communicative and imaginative valence. He repeatedly
affirmed that children need to engage in constant intense activity that
is constructive, elicits their personal involvement, and is in continuous
evolution. Dewey's emphasis on practical work and reflection made him
one of the first to theorise the key value of artistic experiences such as
painting, drawing, modelling, music, drama and play, which in his day
were just beginning to gain acceptance as part of the school curriculum.
One possible approach to implementing this theory was to design labo-
ratories that would foster a virtuous loop between theory and practice.

Similarly, Herbert Read claimed that for the child, reality is a total organic experience, and that educating through art constitutes an integral experience, a means of satisfying the desire for exploration and knowledge. He posited a primitive aesthetic impulse that may be educated and preserved, and that develops, underpinning the need to educate through art and in art.

Read's theories have been used as bases for some teacher training courses that took place between 2015 and 2016 at the Pirelli HangarBicocca centre for contemporary art, in accordance with the educational division (Trovalusci et al., 2017). The chosen exhibits, 'Hypothesis' by Philippe Parreno and 'Doubt' by Carsten Höller, included immersive environments, with numerous sensorial and mental stimulations, that asked for the direct participation of the public. The teachers visited the exhibition before it was totally set up, and art was used as a bridge to experiment many fields that could have then been used with students. At the same time, teachers benefited from the artistic languages, also exploring, living and producing them, thanks to the continuous coming and going from one exhibition setting to another. Living in direct contact with the artistic objects forced the teachers to use different artistic techniques and measure themselves with non-logic and non-linear languages, but complex ones. In this way, they rediscovered the possibilities of investigating and researching. This artistic research, which did not necessary take place with the same artistic language used by the artist, created the opportunity to deepen the possibilities of exploring. Painting, collage, tridimensional constructions, photocollage and photomontage are some of the instruments used to shape thoughts and proposals. The same creative opportunity, lived as a constant search, consequently relapsed on the children involved. As researchers, thanks to the produced material and reflections, to the video and photo documentation, we were given the opportunity to think about the power of research inside a contemporary art centre, in contact with the artwork, behind the scenes of the artwork, while it was being set up. Coming back to the drawings of children, we can observe that they have the characteristics of proper research that uses art in order to investigate and learn about the world. In a number of international contributions (Barrett and Bolt, 2010; Biggs and Karlsson, 2014), the use of art in early childhood education research is a modality used according to different perspectives. Here are some of them: art as an instrument for data collection, as a reflection modality, as an element to reproject, and as a possibility to explore and communicate.

INDIVIDUAL/GROUP TASK

What artistic practices may be used in early childhood education settings? And with what aims in mind?

Art as a method of research in early childhood education

While art may be seen as a process of inquiry in its own right, even when executed for purely artistic purposes, 'art-based research' means something more specific than this. McNiff (2008) has defined it as the 'systematic use of the artistic process, as a primary way of understanding and examining experience' (p. 29). Art-based methods do not merely entail collecting artistic data with a view to analysing them alongside other forms of data. In art-based research, the artistic process itself constitutes the primary mode of inquiry throughout any given study, from the production of the data through sharing the findings. To successfully apply art-based methods, researchers must possess advanced understanding of the artistic process and training in the artistic technique(s) adopted during the research process.

However, for the purposes of this chapter, we hone in on another perspective, known as art-informed research (Knowles and Cole, 2008). In this case, art is viewed as a specific language through which participants can express themselves, facilitating the elicitation of meanings and thoughts that can remain unexpressed when only verbal data are gathered. However, art-informed methods do not only concern the data collection phase; rather, the term 'art-informed' implies a strategic decision on the part of the researcher to adopt a qualitative or mixed method of inquiry (Archibald and Gerber, 2018) that is informed by the arts. To put this another way, it is as though the research method is observed through the filter of the arts.

Children's drawings have long been a focus of research interest, especially in relation to children's cognitive development and their representations of the world (as in Diem-Wille, 2012), and they have also been used to study children's textual comprehension and literacy (as in Kendrick and McKay, 2004). In general, art can offer a privileged mode of inquiry in early childhood education settings, particularly given that children's language ability is still developing during early childhood. The language of art also facilitates work in multicultural settings, where not only is it challenging to communicate verbally with the children, due to their level of development, but also difficulty can arise in communicating with the parents, whose native language, for example, may be different to that of the researcher. In such multilingual contexts, strategically introducing an artistic medium allows thoughts to be translated into a universe that is accessible to both parents and researchers, and in which the children too feel comfortable. Hence, drawing on artistic techniques to enrich one's research method has the potential to become an extremely powerful mode of inquiry within early childhood education settings.

Of course, art in this context is not limited to one expressive form. Rather, the potential, through art, to give voice to multiple and diverse languages and to access different forms of knowledge is of great democratic value in that it accommodates children's 'hundred languages' (Edwards et al., 2012), allowing each individual child to express him or herself. For the teacher, this means giving voice to those who would otherwise remain unheard. The different artistic forms enabling expression of the self and of one's thoughts (not just drawing, but also dance, sculpture, music and song) ensure that the teacher-researcher can reach everyone. This represents a key opportunity, not only in scientific terms, but also at the ethical level, especially in our contemporary era when much of children's learning occurs outside of the educational setting and is in preliterate form (see the influence of digital devices, which are increasingly available to very young children long before they start primary school or learn how to read and write). Advancing our understanding of how children construct knowledge and the most effective strategies for promoting learning means exploring alternative learning processes based on oral, visual and kinaesthetic cultures. In one of her works, Patricia T. Whitfield (2008) warned that concentrating too much on literacy skills, combined with the exclusion of the arts as a learning strategy, risks leading to the exclusion of many children:

Yet, children come to know in a multitude of ways and those whose roots lie in oral, visual or kinaesthetic cultures are placed at a disadvantage when their first experiences with schooling are bereft of joy and individual expression related to their cultural roots.

(p. 153)

The same principle applies to our knowledge of educational strategies in early childhood education. If we only attend to one mode of learning (associated with a given univocal understanding of how this learning is displayed), we risk overlooking all that might come to light on using other forms of exploration. Artistic approaches to research can foster the emergence of other meanings of knowledge, enriching our scientific understanding of early childhood and pointing out alternative forms of thinking.

Within the wide range of possible ways of using art in educational research, we now focus on two potential applications: research with young children and research conducted by teachers/educators on their own professional practice.

INDIVIDUAL/GROUP TASK

How can art and an artistic perspective contribute to research in early childhood education?

Art as a research strategy when working with children

Many authors, including art critics, artists, educationalists, intellectuals and philosophers, have proposed that art is a research strategy in itself. Specifically, the artistic mode of action and reflection facilitates exploration of the complexity and non-linearity of human experience by using preverbal and/or sensory, aesthetic forms of data. It is a process of inquiry engaged in by the artist with a view to illuminating, rather than corroborating or explicating, a given phenomenon. Notably, this perspective on the use of art in research has been made explicit by Graeme Sullivan (2010), who argues that the contemporary world demands an alternative mode of research, one that conserves the complexity of reality, following the logic of transformative practice: '[I realize] that in an uncertain world there is a need to develop more widespread means of exploring human comprehension and that visual arts can play a key role' (p. xxii). Thus, art's inherent potential is attributed with peculiar value as a means of inquiring into our complex contemporary world, which we can never fully observe or understand if we restrict ourselves to a single channel of inquiry, all the less if this channel is binary, logical and rational. Crucially, our use here of the term 'art' is informed by the definition and meaning of art proposed by Herbert Read (1958):

> Art is one of those things that just like the oxygen and the soil are everywhere around us. We almost never think about it, though. That is why art is not something that can be only found in museums and art galleries or in old cities like Florence and Rome. Art, regardless of how we define it, is present in everything we do to please the senses.
>
> (p. 2)

Within the broader paradigm of art as a means of researching complexity, we may make the following specific observation concerning children. Careful observation of their evolving artistic productions in early childhood education settings suggests that in environments that have been meaningfully designed for them by adults, and unless firmly guided by the teacher to strive for likeness, realism or a set outcome, children often try out original approaches to their artwork, exploring previously uncharted territory. Such a tendency may be observed even in the simplest forms of children's artistic expression, such as their drawings. This is the line of inquiry pursued by scholar Claire Golomb (2004) in *Children's Art in Context*. In this work, as penetratingly remarked by Gabriella Gilli (2004), Golomb observed children's drawings and three-dimensional artwork from an interactionist and constructionist perspective, in order not to fall into the risk of absolutising and quantifying the aesthetic perspective. According to the interactionist and constructionist perspective, the production and sharing of artistic artefacts, which has characterised all ages, is a privileged form of 'meaning-making'. It connects the individual mind with the social context, but also the artists and the consumers (Gilli, 2004: vii).

As remarked in the previous paragraph, drawing may be analysed in relation to any or all of its countless potentials, including as a medium for experimentation, exploration and engaging with the challenges of working with the materials. Here, inquiry is not a secondary factor. Indeed, artistic expression that cultivates the dimensions of experimentation and reflection is a key component of the educational event as an instrument of learning (Cahnmann-Taylor and Siegesmund, 2008). However, in formal educational settings such as schools, the potential of art to shed light on subjects' knowledge construction processes is all too frequently underestimated. Conventionally, observation has mainly focused on the reproductive and objective aspects of children's artwork, rather than on the discoveries, divergent perspectives and knowledge transitions inherent in their spontaneous drawings.

An excellent example of putting artistic language at the service of research with children is the mosaic approach (Clark and Moss, 2001), in which intervention is permeated by a spirit of inquiry, and both practitioners and (above all) children are invited to act as researchers. The key purpose here is to receive and record children's thoughts and knowledge about other children (from a 'children about children' perspective), an approach that was applied by Langsted (1994) in the *Children as Citizens* project. For example, inviting children to take photographs allows life in early education to be observed from the children's own perspective: a perspective that the adult, whether teacher or researcher, could not otherwise access, but only formulate hypotheses about. Directly involving the children by deploying the language of photography not only implies recognising the child as competent, but also prompts the adult to be more attentive and to observe things from a different, non-adult perspective (Moran, 2009). When photography is viewed as an artistic language, the aesthetic dimension of a picture becomes an integral part of the research 'data', to be shared and discussed with the children themselves. Independently of what a photograph actually represents, it is the outcome of a process of selecting and producing a particular shot: this process is in itself a form of inquiry that should be valued as part of a broader artistic path.

INDIVIDUAL/GROUP TASK

What educational offerings, and what materials and tools, encourage expressive inquiry on the part of children?

Art as a research strategy for teachers

The work of early education practitioners invariably takes the form of inquiry. These teachers are called to constantly reflect on their own work and actions, and to critically question their own behaviours and interactions with the children. Visual artistic language also serves as a mediator of meanings, enabling educators and teachers to share thoughts and feelings with the children, as well as the rules of everyday life at the early childhood centre (one example is marking cupboards with symbols rather than verbal labels).

Thus, in addition to allowing children to independently explore the meanings of their experiences, and to facilitating researchers' construction of knowledge, art can also inform the ways in which teachers can reflect on their own work. In the words of Eliot Eisner (2002):

> Work in the arts is not only a way of creating performances and products; it is a way of creating our lives by expanding our consciousness, shaping our dispositions, satisfying our quest for thinking, establishing contact with others and sharing a culture.
>
> (p. 3)

An excellent example is the use of artistic languages in pedagogical documentation. Pedagogical documentation itself, when conceptualised as a process of inquiry (Rinaldi, 2006), offers the potential to construct original paths of knowledge that bring into question not only the children's educational experience, but also how practitioners experience their encounter with the children. This in turn enables educators and teachers to revisit their own beliefs and perceptions, thereby adopting a research stance.

For example, collage has been used, within a broader working path, to help early childhood educators explore their representations of the service in which they work and of the role of children (Biffi and Zuccoli, 2016). Since the objective was to work on prejudices, it was decided to use magazines as material. We used very contextualized images in order to address their specific target. The chosen magazines were about science, the house, cooking and animals, but also about motherhood. After the creation of the collages, each participant had the chance to talk about the meaning of their artefact. The collage was able to open metaphorical spaces that allowed the sharing of non-linear and ambiguous meanings that risk remaining implicit or not being fully talked about during a 'traditional' oral discussion.

INDIVIDUAL/GROUP TASK

What does it mean to be teachers/researchers in the field of art?

Conclusion

Art is a method of knowledge gathering in its own right, and as such invites us to reconsider the concepts of method and truth that are so dear to modern science. Perhaps it is for this key reason that it offers a valuable resource to those who wish to immerse themselves in the universe of childhood, a phase of life that is in some respects inaccessible to the gaze of the adult; though adults were once children, they have changed significantly since then. It is precisely adults' recognition of this distance and difference, and at the same time their strong need to access the perspective of the child, that stimulates teachers and researchers to seek strategies and methods for looking at the world with the eyes of a child. Given that it is impossible for adults to gain direct access to the child's point of view, art serves as a transitional space, or transitional dimension, to use the term proposed by Winnicott (1989), facilitating encounter and dialogue, provided, that is, that practitioners are willing to use alternative languages and to humbly set themselves to translating what they have learnt from the scientific universe of shared understanding.

This is surely a complex challenge, but unavoidable if researchers and practitioners truly wish to tap into children's polysemic thinking and the complexity of educational experience. In taking up the challenge, approaches that draw on art represent a valuable resource that has yet to be fully explored.

With regard to the strengths and limitations of art as a research method, it is possible to summarise that:

■ arts can allow the elicitation of inner meanings, but it requires technical competences of the researchers in order to identify the right tecnique based on the participants' skills;

■ arts can support a shared process of knowledge building, but it requires attention in identifying the better form for the dissemination of the results in order to be understood; and

■ arts can be used for enhancing children's engagement, but it requires a high level of attention considering the ethical perspective (avoiding an interpretative and manipulatory approach to the data analysis).

Art as research gives teachers and researchers the possibility to explore reality in a different manner, an open and creative path to explore educational challenges, and the chance to explore languages and proposals actively. This way of looking at the world will relapse onto the children they work with, opening the doors to many rich possibilities:

> The arts have much to offer educational researchers-challenging us to think creatively about what constitutes research; to explore even more varied and creative ways to engage in empirical processes; and to share our questions and findings in more penetrating and widely accessible ways.
>
> (Cahnmann-Taylor, 2008: 4)

Recommended reading

Butler-Kisber, L. (2010) *Qualitative Inquiry: Thematic, Narrative and Arts-Informed Perspectives.* Thousand Oaks, CA: Sage.

Edwards, C., Gandini, L. and Forman, G. (2012) *The Hundred Languages of Children: The Reggio Emilia Experience in Transformation*, 3rd edn. Santa Barbara, CA: Praeger.

Knowles, J.G. and Cole, A. (eds) (2008) *Handbook of the Arts in Qualitative Research: Perspectives, Methodologies, Examples and Issues.* Thousand Oaks, CA: Sage.

References

Archibald, M. and Gerber, N. (2018) Arts and mixed methods research: an innovative methodological merger. *American Behavioral Scientist*, advance online publication, https://doi.org/10.1177/0002764218772672.

Barrett, E. and Bolt, B. (2010) *Practice as Research: Approaches to Creative Arts Enquiry.* London: I.B. Tauris.

Biggs, M. and Karlsson, H. (2014) *The Routledge Companion to Research in the Arts.* London: Routledge.

Biffi, E. and Zuccoli, F. (2016) 'It's not the glue that makes the collage' (Max Erns): training in educational research as an artistic process. In L. Formenti and L. West (eds), *Stories That Make a Difference: Exploring the Collective, Social and Political Potential of Narratives in Adult Education Research.* Lecce: PensaMultimedia, pp. 135–142.

Boone, D.J. (2008) Young children's experience of visual displays of their artwork. *Australian Art Education*, 31(2): 22–45.

Cahnmann-Taylor, M. (2008) Arts-based research: histories and new directions. In M. Cahnmann-Taylor and R. Siegesmund (eds), *Arts-Based Research in Education: Foundations for Practice.* New York: Routledge, pp. 3–15.

Cahnmann-Taylor, M. and Siegesmund, R. (eds) (2008) *Arts-Based Research in Education: Foundations for Practice.* New York: Routledge.

Clark, A. and Moss, P. (2001) *Listening to Young Children: The Mosaic Approach.* London: National Children's Bureau.

Dewey, J. (1995) *Arte come esperienza e altri scritti.* Scandicci: La Nuova Italia.

Diem-Wille, G. (2012) *The Early Years of Life: Psychoanalytical Development Theory According to Freud, Klein, and Bion.* London: Karnac.

Edwards, C., Gandini, L. and Forman, G. (2012) *The Hundred Languages of Children: The Reggio Emilia Experience in Transformation*, 3rd edn. Santa Barbara, CA: Praeger.

Eisner, E. (2002) *Arts and the Creation of Mind.* New Haven, CT: Yale University Press.

Formaggio, D. (1973) *Arte- Enciclopedia filosofica.* Milan: ISEDI.

Gilli, G. (ed.) (2004) *L'arte dei bambini. Contesti culturali e teorie psicologiche.* Milan: Cortina.

Golomb, C. (2004). *L'arte dei bambini. Contesti culturali e teorie psicologiche.* Milan: Raffaello Cortina.

Kendrick, M. and McKay, R. (2004) Drawings as an alternative way of understanding young children's constructions of literacy. *Journal of Early Childhood Literacy*, 4(1): 109–128.

Knowles, J.G. and Cole, A. (eds) (2008) *Handbook of the Arts in Qualitative Research: Perspectives, Methodologies, Examples and Issues.* Thousand Oaks, CA: Sage.

Langsted, O. (1994) Looking at quality from a child's perspective. In P. Moss and A. Pence (eds), *Valuing Quality in Early Childhood Services: New Approaches to Defining Quality.* London: Paul Chapman, pp. 28–42.

McNiff, S. (2008) Art-based research. In J.G. Knowles and A. Cole (eds), *Handbook of the Arts in Qualitative Research: Perspectives, Methodologies, Examples and Issues.* Thousand Oaks, CA: Sage, pp. 29–40.

Moran, M.J. (2009) Indagine collaborativa e uso della fotografia come metodo visuale: un esempio da un programma americano di formazione degli insegnanti. In C.M. Bove (ed.), *Ricerca educativa e formazione. Contaminazioni metodologiche.* Milan: Franco Angeli, pp. 247–271.

Munari, B. (2004) *Fantasia.* Roma-Bari: Editori Laterza.

Read, H. (1958) *Education through Art.* London: Faber & Faber.

Rinaldi, C. (2006) *In Dialogue with Reggio Emilia: Listening, Researching and Learning.* London: Routledge.

Stern, A. (1966) *Arte infantile.* Rome: Armando.

Sullivan, G. (2010) *Art Practice as Research Inquiry in Visual Arts.* Los Angeles, CA: Sage.

Trovalusci, F., Zocco, L. and Zuccoli, F. (2017) Formazione in servizio tra università, scuola e luoghi della cultura: il caso del corso 'Scuola e arte contemporanea: nuove forme di progettazione partecipata'. In P. Magnoler, A.M. Notti and L. Perla (eds), *La professionalità degli insegnanti. La ricerca e le pratiche* (pp. 903–917). Lecce: Pensa MultiMedia.

Twigg, D. and Garvis, S. (2010) Exploring art in early childhood education. *The International Journal of the Arts in Society,* 5(2): 193–204.

Whitfield, P.T. (2008) The heart of the arts: fostering young children's ways of knowing. In M. Narey (ed.), *Making Meaning: Constructing Multimodal Perspectives of Language, Literacy and Learning through Arts-Based Early Childhood Education.* Pittsburgh, PA: Springer, pp. 153–167.

Winnicott, D.W. (1989) *Playing and Reality.* London: Routledge.

Wright, S. (2012) *Children, Meaning-Making and the Arts,* 2nd edn. French Forest, Australia: Pearson Education.

The use of drawing methods with young children in research

5

Helen Lyndon

Introduction

In this chapter, the effectiveness of drawing as a research method with young children is explored. My own research eliciting children's responses using drawing in a variety of ways will be outlined through a discussion around process and outcome. These methods will be placed within a wider methodological context as I explore the research that inspired me to develop and test those drawing methods. The strengths and limitations of the methods will be discussed as I reflect on my own research experiences. The chapter will consider the importance of ethical considerations when researching in such a way with children, particularly as drawing and mark-making forms such a central part of emerging literacy skills.

The context of drawing

Many research methods in use today purport to listen to children's voice, and, with our youngest children, methodological boundaries have been pushed in relation to eliciting drawn responses from children in social research projects.

Drawing as a research methodology with young children has been popular for some time. Kara (2015) suggests that the 'draw and write technique' in educational research has been around since the 1970s, and is a flexible technique that can allow for both qualitative and quantitative analysis as children draw and then describe their image based on a particular stimulus (p. 89). It enables the researcher to 'write' as children 'draw' a response to a prompt and record any discussion that arises. Anning and Ring (2004) were among those earlier twenty-first-century researchers who illustrated the use of young children's drawings as a demonstration of how they construct meaning. They point to the multiple ways that children choose to represent and communicate their growing understanding of the world, and they suggest that children's drawings have the potential to tell us 'much more about childhood than we ever imagined' (p. 124). Their project offered us a difference between creative drawing, which was characteristic of being in a 'state of flow' (similar to that discussed by Csikszentmihalyi, 1997), and representational drawing, which would be more indicative of a landscape artist or an illustrator. Creative drawing offers an emphasis on the process of drawing rather than a focus on an end product. Whatever the definition and purpose of the drawing, such a medium can demonstrate how children were making meaning of their world. Anning and Ring (2004) concluded that multimodality was central to understanding children's preferences as children linked drawing to other playful and creative expressions. They also concluded that drawing represented children's developing understanding of their world.

By understanding children's multimodal communications and accepting that social research can be undertaken through these many voices, researchers demonstrate a pedagogical understanding of the many ways through which children communicate. This is indicative of the work of Loris Malaguzzi and the hundred languages of children (see Edwards et al., 1993), which highlights the many ways in which children can communicate through playing, speaking and listening. By accepting that children can communicate through such a variety of ways, researchers have a duty to explore multiple avenues when seeking children's perspectives. It is important to consider alternatives to standard dialogue, such as drawing and mark-making, and their place within a child's developing skills; children in early education will begin to explore personal expression through mark-making and drawing as a natural part of their development. Early childhood practice strives to encourage such mark-making and drawing in terms of its importance for emerging literacy skills. Drawing therefore offers a developmentally appropriate mechanism through which children's perceptions can be explored.

A paradigm and methodological choice

Using drawing as a research method must first fit into the researcher's underpinning paradigm and methodology choice. Paradigm offers us the wider parameters within which we operate as researchers, and reflects our beliefs about how knowledge is constructed and how knowledge can be sought. The overarching paradigm will determine the methods used later in the research and will influence the answers being sought by the process as a whole (e.g. an interpretivist paradigm seeks interpretation of truth and accepts there can be multiple options, while a positivist paradigm seeks one truth and research often tests hypotheses rather than seeking interpretation). The nature of the data produced through drawing methods is largely qualitative as the drawing often produces a narrative description and interpretation that is central to interpretivist methodologies. That said, it can also be quantified if coding is applied to either the process or end product, thus making it a versatile method (McWhirter et al., 2000); thematic coding (Boyatzis, 1998) can be applied to the drawing of what children love about their setting (e.g. relationships, spaces, activities, objects).

Drawing naturally sits within an interpretivist paradigm (Robson and McCartan, 2016) in which the researcher seeks to interpret an element of the world around them. It also sits well within sociocultural research, which suggests that the social domain in which the child develops influences and informs the child's developing cognition. Through theorists such as Vygotsky (1978), the role of adults and peers are crucial as the child constructs knowledge from their mediated experiences of the world. Drawings can often represent children's emerging understanding of such social relationships, and through discussion this representation can be explored and mapped in detail. Drawing also sits well within a praxeological paradigm (Pascal and Bertram, 2012) as it is a part of typical early education pedagogy and invites the participation of children. Praxeology offers greater participation in the research process than a traditional approach to research, and tries to balance power between researcher and participants, often children, recognising that the child brings their own expertise to the research process.

Drawing can also sit within a range of broader methodological frameworks as researchers secure a comprehensive research design and elicit voice through various methods. Drawing is particularly useful when building up a case study (e.g. Yin, 2018) around a single topic or setting. Case study methodology allows the researcher to build up a picture through a variety of methods around the single case.

Ethical considerations

When undertaking any research with children, there must be strict adherence to ethical guidelines. Notably, obtaining consent from parents and the children themselves, ensuring research is purposeful and worthwhile, and providing feedback to participants are all elements that should be considered (Bertram et al., 2015). As a minimum requirement, a set of ethical guidelines should be adhered to; for research in early education settings, the European Early Childhood Education Research Association (EECERA) ethical guidelines (Bertram et al., 2015) offer sector-specific considerations and consider the multiple modes in which research can be carried out, as well as considerations around preverbal children.

Within any ethical considerations for a project that elicits drawn responses, there should be recognition of the links that drawing as a methodological tool has to drawing and mark-making within typical early education practice. By asking children to participate in a drawing activity, is the researcher asking them to undertake an activity that is usually found within their setting? If this is the case, there should be consideration given to the power relationships that are suggested.

While there is largely a child-centred focus to early education and typically a child-initiated approach to learning within this age range, traditional educational hierarchies remain. In any educational model when an adult asks a child to participate in an activity, there is a danger of the child feeling compelled to do so. It is important that assent as well as consent (Harcourt and Conroy, 2011) becomes a primary ethical consideration. The children should be asked whether they would like to participate in the activity, and then, as the activity unfolds, ongoing consent/assent should be monitored. Children should be able to leave the activity at any point and certainly should not be compelled to 'finish' their drawing.

Most countries recognise children as being under the care and protection of their parents. In the UK, parental consent is required for a child under 16 to participate in an activity within an educational setting.

The law in the UK also recognises, via the Gillick case (United Kingdom House of Lords, 1985), that children should also consent when they sufficiently understand the process that they are to undertake. Children's consent and assent to research has become an ethical absolute and features in ethical research guidelines (BERA, 2018; Bertram et al., 2015).

It is also important that the children understand the purpose of the activity is research, that the researcher is seeking answers regarding the setting or the individual child's preferences. In this vein, it is equally important that the child has some understanding of the purpose and outcomes of the research; where will their drawings go next, and does the child offer their consent for their drawings to be shared with a research community?

A further ethical consideration for anyone researching using drawing is the importance of relationships when working with young children. As already discussed, drawing and mark-marking are part of usual practice within this age group, but progress in this area is dependent upon the relationships that develop. Young children will respond better when they know and trust the adults with whom they work. This makes drawing an optimal medium for the participant or insider researcher who might be undertaking action research with children they already know.

Process and outcome

When utilising drawing methods with young children as a research method, there are thick data within both the process and the outcome of the drawing. As children participate in such an activity, there is the opportunity for discussion and questioning. Dockett et al. (2009) highlight the importance of the drawing process rather than the product, enabling practitioners and researchers the opportunity to dialogue with the child during the drawing experience. The child might explain what they are drawing or the reasons why they have selected to draw such an image; this dialogue can be captured by the researcher through notes and recordings, with appropriate approval and consent, to provide further insight. Researchers should always document the process elements of children's drawings to enrich their data, providing an additional dimension to the analysis and to further validate the conclusions drawn.

The outcome of the drawing also provides data; an image that conveys a child's preference or views on a topic can be coded and classified to contribute to a larger set of data. It too can be annotated with the views and interpretations of the child.

Free drawing

One option for researching with young children is to offer the opportunity for free drawing. Large rolls of paper and a variety of drawing materials provide an invitation or provocation that encourage the children to come and participate in the activity. The role of the researcher here is to sit alongside the children and engage in discussion during this process. The researcher might offer a question as a prompt: 'What do you enjoy about coming to nursery?' 'What are you good at?' 'Tell me about your favourite things . . .' The research might be more specific and participatory in nature, such as asking children what they would like to see in their outdoor environment.

It should be noted that during free drawing experiences, children should be encouraged to participate whatever the outcome; not all children will wish to draw to the prompt, and this can become a disadvantage of this method as much extraneous data are collected. The researcher should also be aware of the fine line between being interested in children's drawing and being intrusive. It is important to recognise that some children may not wish to discuss their drawing.

Free drawing does offer the researcher the opportunity to scrutinise both the process and the outcomes of such drawing. Discussions during the research process can be recorded or reflected upon after the session, and children can also help researchers to annotate such drawings to help illustrate their meaning.

The images below represent free drawing experiences following the prompt 'What do you like about coming to nursery?' I sat alongside a large roll of paper on the floor and asked the children the question as they came over to draw. Figure 5.1 demonstrates a 15-minute interaction within which the child (46 months) explained how the puppet show was used and that 'The Three Little Pigs' was their favourite story to perform; this child discussed how important it was to make the other children sit nicely and listen to the show. The child explained that they used a squeaky voice for the pigs and they sounded mean when they were the wolf. They asked me to annotate the illustration with 'I like to play with the puppet show'. This drawn response is representational in that the child wanted to illustrate the puppet show, yet the discussion process revealed a rich description about why the activity was preferential.

Figure 5.2 demonstrates an interaction of just under five minutes in which the child joined me during a very quiet period. This child initially chose to ignore the prompt and start mark-making with a black crayon; this was followed by a brief discussion about what the child enjoyed. They expressed how much they enjoyed playing at home with Mummy and Daddy, and asked me to annotate 'Mummy and Daddy are not at preschool'. When practitioners later reflected upon this illustration, they discussed the transitional issues that this child was having and discussed how this could be better managed.

Free drawing experiences in this research were analysed by practitioners who found that most of the illustrations children drew were around friends and family. This was similar to previous research, which concluded that relationships were of key importance to children at this age (Clark and Moss, 2011).

Figure 5.1 Free drawing (i)

Figure 5.2 Free drawing (ii)

Drawing as part of map-making

Map-making was first described as part of Clark and Moss's (2011) mosaic approach, during which children were asked to compile a map of their setting. They used both digital images and drawing to compile a map that invariably contained places and spaces of significance to the child. This purposeful approach to drawing provides some structure that might help children in formulating a response. Once constructed, the maps can then be utilised further in the research process as the child can offer a tour of the setting and explain to the researcher the different aspects on the map.

Figure 5.3 demonstrates a drawing by a child of 36 months who was answering the prompt 'Where do you like to play?' While the rest of the group were drawing parts of the nursery space, this child thought about the places he was taken by his parents. This interaction was on a one-to-one basis and lasted only eight minutes; the child expressed their favourite place to play as the local playground, particularly the 'monkey bars'. On these, the child could show he was strong and hold on for a long time.

Figure 5.3 Map-making

The maps that were made by the children in this research were analysed thematically; most children had illustrated something outdoors and many had discussed adventures that they had experienced with friends and family.

Drawing within a graduated framework

Drawing within a given framework offers the researcher the opportunity to ask the children for a graduated response. Eldén (2012) used concentric circles of closeness to research the relationship children have with their carers, offering a graduated response in terms of attachments to the child. The resulting drawing represented a complex set of connected relationships that demonstrated both practical care and emotional support. This model of concentric circles can be utilised to ask children to respond to any prompt as each level of the circle represents the preferences of the child. In my own research, concentric circles were explored as providing a means of eliciting a graduated response from children; the children were asked to place their favourite in the centre and their least favourite around the outside. The observation of this process and the dialogue that resulted was captured and formed part of the data.

In the illustrations below, children were asked to consider their educational visit to a local zoo. The children were given three concentric circles that provided four spaces for their preferences, including the outside of the diagram. I introduced the drawing activity the day after the educational visit, and explained that the activity was out on the table and they were all welcome to come and participate throughout the session. A tabletop space for up to three children, plus myself, was set aside. The children were keen to participate as relationships with the researcher were already established.

Figure 5.4, completed by a child of 40 months, demonstrates their preferences on the trip. Their favourite part of the day was seeing the tiger and they enjoyed much of the day, and so did not want to draw anything in the outside circle. This child discussed their day with the researcher for almost 40 minutes as they articulated the experience of travelling with friends on the coach 'with seatbelts that go click'; this had been their first experience of group coach travel. The child was very clear about their preferences and was happy to draw selected elements. This child also took the opportunity to explain the process to the other children around the table and directed the researcher to label their diagram 'You have to put the things you don't like around here'.

Figure 5.5 demonstrates the participation of a child who claimed to be unable to draw. They were happy to undertake the discussion around their own preferences but were reluctant to draw the elements discussed. What was striking about this discussion was the inclusion of an additional circle that was drawn by the child to demonstrate their preferences: 'Snack time was more fun than seeing the lion, but it was good too'. Equally, this child had not enjoyed walking around the spaces within the zoo as there had been some steep hills, and this was articulated using the outside spaces of the circles.

As the children completed their concentric circles and engaged in discussions with me about their day trip, practitioners observed elements of the dialogue to feed back to the leadership team and parents regarding the success of the day.

Here, the options for children's participation are broad as they might be asked to respond to a whole range of issues. The resulting drawing represented a complex set of connected relationships that demonstrated both practical care and emotional support.

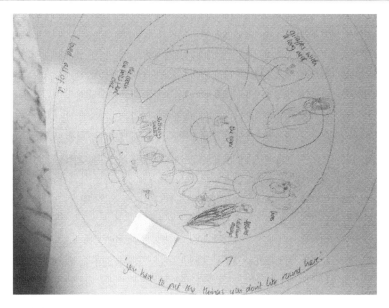

Figure 5.4 Concentric circles (i)

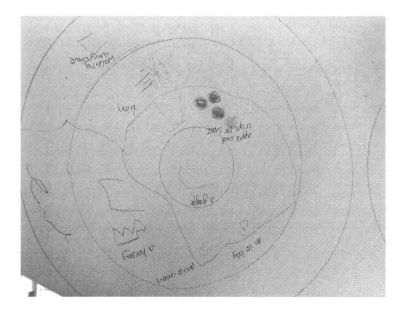

Figure 5.5 Concentric circles (ii)

The concentric drawings in this case were analysed by practitioners who concluded that while the children enjoyed the obvious experiences of seeing the animals, they also valued the interactions with their peers during the day. Graduated responses of this type could also be analysed numerically, with each section of the diagram holding a value; further exploration of this method is needed to fully explore the possibilities.

Strengths of the detailed research methods

- The open-ended nature of the tasks invite children to participate at their own developmental level.

- It fits easily into typical early childhood practice and is ideal for practitioner research.

- The room for dialogue provides rich data in terms of process and outcome.

- The methods encourage children's participation in their education and care, and provide a voice that can be used in evaluation of services.

Limitations of the detailed research methods

- Vast amounts of data can be generated and children from 'outside' the research group might choose to participate.

- Some children already have a perception that they are unable to draw and may opt out.

- Participatory interpretation requires time and space but is essential in full interpretation of the drawn responses.

Summary

Drawing as a research method can take many forms and offers versatility as it can provide data in its production as well as its outcome. It provides a natural and developmentally appropriate way of seeking the views and ideas of young children, which can be elicited with careful consideration of the ethical implications.

Recommended reading

Harcourt, D., Perry, B. and Waller, T. (2011) *Researching Young Children's Perspectives*. London: Routledge.

Kara, H. (2015) *Creative Research Methods in the Social Sciences: A Practical Guide*. Bristol: Policy Press.

References

Anning, A. and Ring, K. (2004) *Making Sense of Children's Drawings*. Maidenhead: Open University Press.

Bertram, T., Formosinho, J., Gray, C., Pascal, C. and Whalley, M. (2015) *EECERA Code for Early Childhood Researchers*. Available at: www.eecera. org/wp-content/uploads/2016/07/EECERA-Ethical-Code.pdf (accessed 11 December 2018).

Boyatzis, R.E. (1998) *Transforming Qualitative Information: Thematic Analysis and Code Development*. London: Sage.

British Education Research Association (BERA) (2018) *Ethical Guidelines for Educational Research*, 4th edn. Available at: www.bera.ac.uk/ wp-content/uploads/2018/06/BERA-Ethical-Guidelines-for-Educational-Research_4thEdn_2018.pdf?noredirect=1 (accessed 11 December 2018).

Clark, A. and Moss, P. (2011) *Listening to Young Children: The Mosaic Approach*. London: National Children's Bureau.

Csikszentmihalyi, M. (1997) *Finding Flow: The Psychology of Engagement with Everyday Life*. New York: Basic Books.

Dockett, S., Einarsdottir, J. and Perry, B. (2009) Researching with children: ethical tensions. *Journal of Early Childhood Research*, 7(3): 283–298.

Edwards, C., Gandini, L. and Foreman, G. (1993) *The Hundred Languages of Children: The Reggio Emilia Approach to Early Childhood Education*. Westport, CT: Ablex.

Eldén, S. (2012) Inviting the messy: drawing methods and children's voices. *Childhood*, 20(1): 66–81.

Harcourt, D. and Conroy, H. (2011) Informed consent. In D. Harcourt, B. Perry and T. Waller (eds), *Researching Young Children's Perspectives*. London: Routledge, pp. 38–51.

Kara, H. (2015) *Creative Research Methods in the Social Sciences*. Bristol: Policy Press.

McWhirter, J.M., Collins, M., Bryant, I., Wetton, N.M. and Newton-Bishop, J. (2000) Evaluating 'Safe in the Sun': a curriculum programme for primary schools. *Health Education Research*, 15(2): 203–217.

Pascal, C. and Bertram, T. (2012) Praxis, ethics and power: developing praxeology as a participatory paradigm for early childhood research. *The European Early Childhood Research Association Journal*, 20(4): 477–492.

Robson, C. and McCartan, K. (2016) *Real World Research*, 4th edn. Chichester: Wiley.

United Kingdom House of Lords (1985) *Gillick v West Norfolk and Wisbech Area Health Authority*. AC 112 of 17 October 1985. Available at: www.bailii. org/uk/cases/UKHL/1985/7.html (accessed 4 March 2019).

Vygotsky, L.S. (1978) *Mind in Society: The Development of Higher Psychological Processes*. Cambridge, MA: Harvard University Press.

Yin, R.K. (2018) *Case Study Research and Applications: Design and Methods*. London: Sage.

Listening to young children in messy, playful research

Laura Heads and Michael Jopling

In early childhood research, multi-method approaches such as the 'mosaic approach' (Clark and Moss, 2011) are popular for listening to young children's perspectives. However, there appears to be a developing interest in diversifying listening approaches, including using children's own playfulness and creativity to support multiple expressions of voice (e.g. Blaisdell et al., 2018). Similarly, there have previously been calls for researchers to move beyond method (Law, 2004) and engage in 'messy methodologies', which value complexity over certainty and create playful spaces for children and researchers to operate in ambiguous ways (Rautio, 2013). With this context in mind, we offer a reflective account of part of Laura's PhD research, which mobilised a playful methodology inspired by Deleuze and Guattari's theoretical work to investigate how reception children's ideas could be used to problematise narrow conceptualisations of 'school readiness'. Inspiration for the playful approach was sparked by some data created by a child during a preliminary study in the research. We suggest that this drawing of a classroom (see Figure 6.1) captured something of the complex and emergent nature of both life and learning in an early years classroom, as well as the messy, indeterminate process that is researching with children. Additionally, the rhizomatic form of the drawing helped steer the research in the direction of post-structuralist theory to support the development of a method, which we hoped would acknowledge the spontaneous emergence and intelligent nature of reception children's ideas.

INDIVIDUAL/GROUP TASK

As you read, think about how theory could stimulate your own creative and playful approaches to researching with young children.

The drawing in Figure 6.1 was a stimulus that led to a more open, playful approach to the research. The constrained responses of professionals to it prompted the need to engage young children as a starting point, rather than attempting to adapt existing methods or meet preconceived outcomes. In this, we were guided by theoretical insights from Deleuze and Guattari (1987), who asserted: 'Contrary to a deeply rooted belief, the book is not an image of the world. It forms a rhizome with the world, there is an aparallel evolution of the book and the world' (p. 12). This chapter is founded on the understanding that it is not an image of the research it describes, and, while it is tempting to draw parallels between researcher and research in areas such as the struggles with articulation, the development of a voice, and the challenges of interpretation, it is just as important to recognise the 'aparallels': the refusal

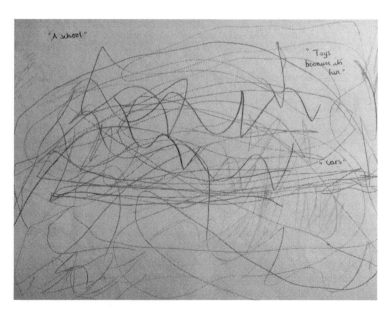

Figure 6.1 Messy, playful encounters

of the 'data' to remain fixed, and the enduring messiness that makes the process of research so challenging and rewarding.

INDIVIDUAL/GROUP TASK

How might the drawing in Figure 6.1 relate to your experiences of researching or working with young children? Might you have jumped to the same conclusion as the teachers about the child's 'unreadiness' for school?

Ideas Club: messy, playful research

The specific study on which this chapter focuses is an after-school 'Ideas Club', a playful and emergent research space in which Laura spent time with small groups of eight reception children (aged 4 and 5 years old) from three schools in North East England for an hour a week, over a four-week period. The decision to focus on reception children's ideas was to explore 'school readiness' policy and the perceived importance of reception children's 'readiness' for Year 1, a year group that marks the start of the National Curriculum (Department for Education, 2013) and more formal learning. The after-school study was named 'Ideas Club' to raise the status of children's ideas and to engage with children in ways that resisted the measurement and comparison of children as subjects, as is commonplace in educational policy and practice.

The after-school club approach was influenced by Bailey (2016), who carried out a year-long ethnographic study of a school-based *Minecraft* club, examining how a group of individuals interacted while engaging in virtual world play. Bailey's (2016) use of the phrases 'club community' and 'club participants' invoked feelings of belonging and collaboration, and the challenge was to see if a similar ethos could be cultivated by using an after-school club approach with reception children. Thinking more seriously about using an after-school club, Laura also drew on her experiences of running extracurricular activities as a teacher, such as a film club and a handball club. While after-school clubs are not wholly free from school expectations and associations, they are usually more informal in atmosphere, and offer a valuable time to talk and play beyond the 'official' school day. Reflecting on these experiences suggested that an after-school club might allow time and space to be more autonomous, more open-ended and slower in approach (Horton and Kraftl, 2006), compared to carrying out a study during the school day.

The development of these methods was influenced by a range of studies that had used the work of Deleuze and Guattari to develop methodological approaches for working with children (e.g. Davies, 2014; Hollett and Ehret, 2015; Sellers, 2013). This made it clear that paying special attention to the body and its connections with the material world should be valued as key parts of the research process (Clark, 2011; Woodyer, 2008). It may be that research with young children is more amenable to this kind of attention to slowness and physicality, which was a conscious response to what were regarded as the methodological compromises of the preceding preliminary study. However, this was also an area in which the needs of the research were aparallel with the pressure to complete it to deadline.

The importance of generating an 'affective' research atmosphere by using a wide range of resources was also clear. Resources used included picture books, such as *What Is a Child?* (Alemagna, 2018), and play-based provisions, such as clay and junk materials. The concept of 'affect' is central to Deleuzo-Guattarian philosophy, and was mobilised in this research as a perceived 'momentary intensity' (Massumi, 1995) or 'felt focal moment' (Ehret et al., 2016) that transforms thinking. It was by drawing on Deleuzo-Guattarian concepts such as 'rhizome' and 'affect' that the research could mobilise the view that children and researchers can work together in more lively, playful and experimental ways than are usually expected, a process that also helped reconceptualise the notion of 'school readiness'. Moreover, the difficulty of describing Ideas Club reflects the challenge of undertaking open-ended, participatory research. While the temptation was there to force the pace and organise activities that seemed more likely to provide 'useful' data, resisting this required a holding of the nerve to trust the indeterminacy of the approach and allow the children's voices to emerge without coercion.

An affective, multisensory methodology

The affective, playful methodology adopted was designed to reflect the post-structuralist underpinnings of the research, to engage reception children in ways that would capture and inspire their intelligence and creativity, and to provoke new thinking about 'school readiness'. While children participated in some pre-planned activities, as already indicated the approach was imbued with 'slowness' (Horton and Kraftl, 2006) and flexibility, understanding that knowledge about 'school readiness' was not there to be uncovered, but would likely be generated by the group in unexpected ways during our sessions. Given this open-ended approach, it is therefore difficult to offer a simple, replicable account of Ideas Club, given that the methods used were so fluid and resistant to straighforward replication. However, Figure 6.2 gives a flavour of the kinds of materials that were used to faciliate Ideas Club sessions. The following section also offers accounts of children's use of clay and junk materials, which indicate the kinds of affective, multisensory encounters that helped to challenge existing notions of 'school readiness'.

Aside from the concepts of Deleuze and Guattari, inspiration for these methods also came in other forms, such as the creative methodologies of Gauntlett (2007), who has worked on helping people communicate ideas about their lives through 'making things' (e.g. using Lego, collage and video) and reflecting on the process. Gauntlett (2007) emphasises that playful and imaginative methodologies can prompt a different, more reflexive kind of engagement from participants than talk-based methods, such as focus groups and interviews, which often capture 'instant descriptions' of participants' views. This suggested that making things hands-on as part of an after-school approach might allow Reception children time to apply their 'playful and creative intention'

- Open-ended exploration of clay.

- Junk material challenges.

- Using drawing as a response to picture books.

- Using 'mini-mes' – photographs of the children cut out and added to lollypop sticks to use as puppets in open-ended play.

- Snack time – a time for children to sit as a group and chat informally.

Figure 6.2 Ideas Club methods

(Gauntlett, 2007) and stimulate more thoughtful reflection. The idea that children could be given time to play and make things also felt like a suitable way of reflecting and respecting the interests of young children, many of whom had described their enjoyment of using Lego and art materials in the preceding study.

Using clay and junk materials as research tools

One of the most significant of the Ideas Club encounters can be seen in Figure 6.3 in the image entitled 'The Pearl and the Platform'. Clay was used in different ways during Ideas Club. The children were motivated to use clay for much longer periods when they were exploring and experimenting for their own purposes. One child used the clay to make a model of their family. Another child used their thumb to press 'rabbit holes' into the clay. The clay model in Figure 6.3 felt particularly important, given the highly imaginative narrative the child produced independently of adult-driven outcomes, which sits uneasily with narrow interpretations of 'school readiness' and simple models of early literacy.

A further example of children's ingenuity with materials can be seen in the images in Figure 6.4. In the first session, each child was given a plastic straw, a pipe cleaner, a paper cupcake case and some masking tape as a starting point for enquiry. Each of the 24 children across the three schools used these materials in a different way. Finished objects included

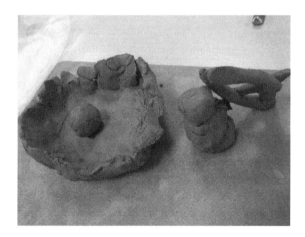

*I've made a platform with a
beautiful pearl. It's a bed
for the pearl.*

*This is a little pearl that's
been cracked open.*

*And this was little special
pearl, that lived on the beach,
but then it, someone pushed
it down and it fell into here.*

*And this is a bow and
arrow and this man is
holding the bow and
arrow to take care of
the pearl.*

Figure 6.3 'The Pearl and the Platform'

Figure 6.4 Objects

a fishing rod, a vacuum cleaner and a magic wand. Asking children to explore these materials prompted arbitrary yet curious conversation. It also indicated how open-ended activity can evoke feelings of enjoyment and frustration. At the time of Ideas Club, 'fidget spinners' were a popular craze – recognisable as a palm-sized spinning toy made from metal or plastic. One of the children asked if we could make our own fidget spinners, and so we did, using milk bottle tops and other materials. Important to note here is the child-led nature of this activity and the importance of valuing the children's input throughout Ideas Club.

As a sensory experience, Ideas Club felt like clay and junk materials in our hands and between our fingers, it sounded like laughter and talk, and the crunch of biscuits in our mouths, and it looked like fidget spinners, cardboard box classrooms and picture books. Ideas Club also felt, looked and sounded different in each of the three schools involved in the research, reflecting the unique collectivity of children who took part in each club. The 'interfering charge' of affect and emergence (Massumi, 2002) made each Ideas Club session a unique and indeterminate experience, in that the children connected with each other, the materials, and Laura herself in abstract ways that could not be predetermined or replicated in other schools.

INDIVIDUAL/GROUP TASK

Can you use the explorations described here to inspire children to develop their own ideas? How would you analyse or evaluate what they gain from such approaches?

Analysis

As a result of engaging with post-structuralism, Laura came to reject the separation of data into boxes (St. Pierre, 2013) and the 'artificial neatness' (Strom et al., 2014) of traditional qualitative analysis. Instead, the research focused on the 'affective' elements of the children's ideas, and the ideas that sparked new pathways. For example, the 'Pearl and the Platform' story (see Figure 6.3) prompted more detailed consideration of how far sensory learning experiences are reflected in the Year 1 curriculum. This more 'affective' approach to analysis was informed by Leander and Rowe's (2006) 'rhizo-analysis', the 'ideas tracing' of Ehret et al. (2016), and MacLure's (2013) notion of 'potentiality' – being open to data that 'glows'.

Reflections

Many of the reflections on the Ideas Club process were concerned with the children's levels of engagement during the sessions and the challenge of trying to overcome the temptation to predetermine the activities to ensure 'useful' data were generated and collected. Similar challenges were described by Blaisdell et al. (2018), who also took an open-ended approach to working with young children:

> In our piloting, we were keen to establish ways of working with children that centered their own creativity and play, shaped by the materials we provided but not directed by us. However, [. . .] we struggled to balance our own agenda with the more open-ended methods we had used.
>
> (p. 14)

During the study, it was noticeable that children's engagement was markedly greater when they were given the opportunity to experiment with materials, such as clay, on their own terms, favouring the process of learning rather than fixed outcomes. During one session, children audibly groaned when they were told they would be set a 'challenge', which was taken as a signal to let them pursue their own experimentation. Gradually, Laura became more sensitised to seeing children's meaning-making in new ways, and found that the intelligence and creativity of reception children was best captured not through questioning, but by being present in the narratives and objects they produced and imagined. This underlined the fact that knowledge is more fluid and changeable, especially among young children, than is often recognised. Importantly, it also became apparent in 'listening' to children that there is a danger that as researchers, we only hear certain things, in much the same way as a teacher might only listen to children for evidence of specific learning outcomes. This is where audio recordings played a vital role. Listening to the audio revealed elements and meanings in children's ideas that were not clear in real time. The implications of this are significant for both researchers and teachers. For example, how much of children's intelligence do we miss when we only listen in a particular way?

Overall, the term 'listening' came to feel like an inadequate way of describing the research process, given the playfulness and creativity of the research approach. 'Multisensory listening', such as that described by Clark (2005), also felt lacking as a term, as such approaches are linked to helping children 'articulate their knowledge'. In contrast, the research endeavoured to use movement and play to listen to children in ways that allowed the 'not-yet-known to emerge' (Davies, 2014). Notions of emergence and intra-activity (Barad, 2003) came to extend the definition of listening, which guided the research: 'Listening is about being open to being affected [. . .] Listening is about not being bound by what you already know. It is life as movement' (Davies, 2014: 1).

INDIVIDUAL/GROUP TASK

Think about how you would experiment with different ways of listening to children. How would you use what you learn?

Finally, the children's high expectations of Ideas Club in terms of their enjoyment should be highlighted; after all, after-school clubs are supposed to be fun. One child was disappointed not to have done any 'exploding rocket experiments' in Ideas Club; another just wanted to 'play in the classroom'. Such expectations expose the difference between after-school club research contexts and more traditional 'in-school' approaches, as well as the indeterminacy that we should accept is central to playful, open-ended research. There are parallels and aparallels here with the research process itself. It was vital again to trust that this mutually reinforcing approach led by both researcher and children would produce more interesting and authentic data than more traditional methods. Key to this was recognising that theory and methods also operated interdependently: theory was applied because it was appropriate as a way of investigating school readiness through listening to young children, not to impress or because it was expected. Aparallels related to the need to restrict the messy and playful creation of knowledge in order to make it fit as data with the temporal and formal restrictions of PhD research. Researchers adopting similar approaches must therefore think about how they reconcile their research aims with children's agendas and wishes, and be aware of the potentially revolutionary effect of listening attentively to children: 'If little children managed to make their protests heard in nursery school, or even simply their questions, it would be enough to derail the whole education system' (Deleuze, 2004: 208).

Strengths of this approach

- Open-ended, playful approaches allow children to make connections in unexpected ways. Open-ended, playful engagement with children led to unexpected yet highly valuable data, which challenge received wisdoms about 'school readiness'.

- Adopting a playful approach created a more inclusive research experience for the children, particularly as the methods appeared to reflect and respect the children's interests.

- The playful methodology supported a reflective, affective approach and allowed for multiple expressions of voice.

Limitations of this approach

- As Blaisdell et al. (2018) found, open-ended research cannnot be guaranteed to produce the data you are looking for, particularly if you are exploring children's perspectives on specific topics. This can be discomforting for researchers used to more traditional methods.

- Adopting an open-ended, playful approach raises unique ethical issues linked to consent. This is because it is hard to specify in advance for children or parents the precise details of the methods that will be used. Also, in this research, some children were disappointed that they could not take part in the club due to other after-school commitments.

■ The data produced through messy methodologies are likely to produce messy, complex data. Researchers will therefore need to explore alternative ways of analysing such data.

Conclusion

It was only part way through the research that the value of 'plugging into theory' (Jackson and Mazzei, 2012) became apparent. Plugging into a post-structuralist framework helped to challenge taken-for-granted knowledge relating to 'school readiness', to embrace the 'mess' in social science research (Law, 2004), and to work with children in a slower, more playful way than we had previously thought possible. The challenge was to maintain the risk-taking that is central to innovation, but often more rhetorical than real, and to trust that theory would underpin the more open, playful methods to which it was leading. We hope Ideas Club helps you to think about how you could make the research process slower and more creative to accommodate the complexity of young children's lives. This requires us to accept that researching with children will never be a neat, logical process. Children are spontaneous and intelligent beings who respond to the world around them in uniquely perceptive, changeable ways, and they deserve innovative approaches that recognise this. Certainly, it should not have been surprising that the child's drawing illustrated in Figure 6.1 would provide the inspiration and clarity necessary to expand the research approach, having worked with so many intelligent young children. Yet it did, and this is why children's ideas offer great hope in helping all of us think differently about the world, so long as we are also prepared to research differently:

> If the world is complex and messy, then at least some of the time we're going to have to give up on simplicities. But one thing is sure: if we want to think about the messes of reality at all then we're going to have to teach ourselves to think, to practice, to relate, and to know in new ways.
>
> (Law, 2004: 2)

Summary

■ Researching with young children can be a messy and complex process. Using open and playful methodologies helped support and celebrate this complexity.

■ Using an after-school club as a research context offered the time and space to 'slow down' and explore the complexities of young children's lives in more detail.

■ Theory prompted the development of more creative, open-ended methods, compared to the preliminary study.

■ Using an open-ended approach is not easy. Trusting the indeterminacy of the approach helped allow the children's voices to emerge without coercion.

■ Picture books, clay and junk materials are useful tools for promoting a creative approach to researching with young children.

Acknowledgements

We would like to acknowledge the extensive contribution of Dr Charmaine Agius Ferrante to the research drawn on in this chapter.

Recommended reading

Jackson, A.Y. and Mazzei, L.A. (2012) *Thinking with Theory in Qualitative Research.* London: Routledge.

Law, J. (2004) *After Method: Mess in Social Science Research.* London: Routledge.

Sellers, M. (2013) *Young children Becoming Curriculum: Deleuze, Te Whāriki and Curricular Understandings.* London: Routledge.

References

Alemagna, B. (2018) *What Is a Child?* London: Tate Publishing.

Bailey, C. (2016) Free the sheep: improvised song and performance in and around a minecraft community. *Literacy*, 50(2): 62–71.

Barad, K. (2003) Posthumanist performativity: toward an understanding of how matter comes to matter. *Signs: Journal of Women in Culture and Society*, 28(3): 801–831.

Blaisdell, C., Arnott, L., Wall, K. and Robinson, C. (2018) Look who's talking: using creative, playful arts-based methods in research with young children. *Journal of Early Childhood Research*, 1–18. (OnlineFirst), https://doi.org/10.1177/147 6718X18808816.

Clark, A. (2005) Listening to and involving young children: a review of research and practice. *Early Child Development and Care*, 175(6): 489–505.

Clark, A. (2011) Multimodal map making with young children: exploring ethnographic and participatory methods. *Qualitative Research*, 11(3): 311–330.

Clark, A. and Moss, P. (2011) *Listening to Young Children: The Mosaic Approach*, 2nd edn. London: National Children's Bureau.

Davies, B. (2014) *Listening to Children: Being and Becoming*. London: Routledge.

Deleuze, G. (2004) *The Logic of Sense*. London: Continuum.

Deleuze, G. and Guattari, F (1987) *A Thousand Plateaus*. Minneapolis, MN: University of Minnesota Press.

Department for Education (2013) *The National Curriculum in England: Key Stages 1 and 2 Framework Document*. Available at: www.gov.uk/govern ment/publications/national-curriculum-in-england-primary-curriculum (accessed 20 October 2018).

Ehret, C., Hollett, T. and Jocius, R. (2016) The matter of new media making: an intra-action analysis of adolescents making a digital book trailer. *Journal of Literacy Research*, 48(3): 346–377.

Gauntlett, D. (2007) *Creative Explorations: New Approaches to Identity and Audience*. London: Routledge.

Hollett, T. and Ehret, C. (2015) 'Bean's World': (Mine)crafting affective atmospheres of gameplay, learning, and care in a children's hospital. *New Media & Society*, 17(11): 1849–1866.

Horton, J. and Kraftl, P. (2006) What else? Some more ways of thinking and doing 'children's geographies'. *Children's Geographies*, 4(1): 69–95.

Jackson, A.Y. and Mazzei, L.A. (2012) *Thinking with Theory in Qualitative Research*. London: Routledge.

Law, J. (2004) *After Method: Mess in Social Science Research*. London: Routledge.

Leander, K.M. and Rowe, D.W. (2006) Mapping literacy spaces in motion: a rhizomatic analysis of a classroom literacy performance. *Reading Research Quarterly*, 41(4): 428–460.

MacLure, M. (2013) The wonder of data. *Cultural Studies, Critical Methodologies*, 13(4): 228–232.

Massumi, B. (1995) The autonomy of affect. *Cultural Critique*, 31: 83–109.

Massumi, B. (2002) *Parables for the Virtual: Movement, Affect, Sensation*. Durham, NC: Duke University Press.

Rautio, P. (2013) Children who carry stones in their pockets: on autotelic material practices in everyday life. *Children's Geographies*, 11(4): 394–408.

Sellers, M. (2013) *Young Children Becoming Curriculum: Deleuze, Te Whāriki and Curricular Understandings*. London: Routledge.

St. Pierre, E.A. (2013) The appearance of data. *Cultural Studies, Critical Methodologies*, 13(4): 223–227.

Strom, K., Abi-Hanna, R., Dacey, C. and Duplaise, J. (2014) Exploring and connecting lines of flight. In M. Taylor and L. Coia (eds), *Gender, Feminism, and Queer Theory in the Self-Study of Teacher Education Practices*. Rotterdam: Sense Publishing, pp. 31–44.

Woodyer, T. (2008) The body as research tool: embodied practice and children's geographies. *Children's Geographies*, 6(4): 349–362.

Play-based interview techniques with young children

Sarah Holmes

Introduction

This chapter will explore the method of play-based interviews, which is a highly effective tool for use among young children that takes into account their cognitive and language limitations. This approach facilitates each interview to be tailored to the child, while enabling consistency of data collection. Guidance on designing and tailoring the research tool is provided, alongside example activities. This chapter will also detail some of the strengths and limitations of this research method, including the challenges of interviewing young children.

The value of interviewing children

Interviews are a good way to find out first-hand the thoughts, feelings or ideas of children. While consulting the views of others *about* a child can be very enlightening, many researchers find that speaking *with* the child directly reveals more interesting and valuable data for research projects (Greig and Taylor, 1999; Prior, 2016). In an interview, the researcher is able to ask about the precise area of interest, rather than being reliant on the observations or reports of second-hand sources of data about the child. Furthermore, it is possible to probe for reasons behind the child's answer in an interview in a way that is not possible if tools such as surveys, questionnaires or naturalistic observations are employed (O'Kane, 2008). Interviews can be flexible and dynamic, responding to the answers of the participant, which aids the quality and depth of the research findings. If implemented correctly, the child feels valued and affirmed through having the opportunity of being interviewed (Prior, 2016). There can therefore be great value in interviewing children.

The challenges of conventional interview methods with young children

There are increased challenges when interviewing young children. Since this chapter particularly considers research with children around 3 to 6 years old, it is important to be aware of their varied and emerging verbal abilities. A young child may not be able to effectively express using words their genuine, deep-rooted thoughts, feelings or ideas (Prior, 2016). Therefore, the researcher cannot assume that what is verbalised in an interview context is a full demonstration of the child's thinking, feelings or cognitive understanding. In addition, the process of memory construction, organisation and retrieval is highly complex (Quinn, 2014), and the child's responses can often be erroneous in an artificial interview context. An example of this is that the tasks and experimental context of Piaget (1967) have been heavily criticised for being so different to a child's normal everyday experience, resulting in children finding them difficult to relate to and understand, and consequently making it impossible for young children to reveal their true competences (Donaldson, 1978). Furthermore, a young child's attention span often impacts upon the ability to sustain an interview, particularly if traditional interview styles are adopted. Children's responses may also be impacted by their wariness of the adult researcher leading them to say what they perceive the researcher expects or desires (Prior, 2016). Indeed, Bunge (2006) questioned the ability to hear the child's authentic and true voice in conversations because young children are vulnerable and naturally seek to please adults. This effect may be further increased if parents are present because family members often seek to present a harmonious front to outsiders (Mayall, 2001). The purpose of the play-based interview research method is therefore to reduce the impact of these challenges, enabling more natural responses to be obtained from participants.

INDIVIDUAL/GROUP TASK

What contexts/settings/activities do you know of where children would feel relaxed and comfortable to respond naturally and therefore more genuinely to a researcher? Would any of these situations be appropriate for your research to take place in? How can you seek to create a comfortable environment for participants during your research?

Play-based interview techniques

Research design

This method incorporates ideas of semi-structured interviewing (Prior, 2016), participatory methods (O'Kane, 2001) and creative methodologies (Winter, 2016), alongside awareness of early childhood education professional practice. It entails devising a range of play-based tasks and activities to permit the observation of the target traits, actions or behaviours in young children. Once the research aims have been clearly formulated (Greig et al., 2013), the researcher's early childhood experience and skill may be employed to devise activities that are age-appropriate, interesting and engaging for the child, while revealing the desired aspects in a way that may be documented and analysed methodically. This may include role play with puppets, discussing pictures together (see Figure 7.4), or modelling using Play-Doh, bricks or drawing.

INDIVIDUAL/GROUP TASK

What resources and skills do you have that could be utilised within play-based interviews? How could these skills and resources be developed to achieve your research aims and facilitate high-quality research with your target sample? Are there any gaps in your skills that you could consider resourcing from elsewhere?

Aligning with the notion of doing research *with* rather than *on* children (O'Kane, 2001), it is good practice to encourage the child to shape the agenda of the play-based interview (Clark et al., 2013). This occurs by designing a portfolio of tasks in conjunction with the research aims in advance of the interview. The researcher takes all necessary resources for these activities to the interview setting, enabling the child to choose which activities interest them. This may be somewhat directed by the researcher in order to achieve the research aims, (e.g. to offer the child the choice of Play-Doh or building blocks, both of which could be utilised to discuss the child's family relationships). Alternatively, the researcher could describe briefly at the beginning of the interview the four activities that they have brought and allow the child to choose the order and pace of them. For example, in a project investigating friendships, a child may choose to spend most of the time drawing a picture of their friends, while they discuss issues pertinent to the research aims, and then only spend a few minutes towards the end taking part in role play using a puppet to discuss sharing. Equally, the researcher may find that a child becomes so enthralled in one activity that they are able to raise all of the target aspects with the child during that activity, so that no subsequent tasks are required and the interview is complete. In most situations, the researcher will need to partake in three or four of the portfolio activities in order to gain insight into all of the research aims. The key is to be flexible and allow each interview to be individually formed in a partnership between the researcher and the child. A well-designed and well-thought-through portfolio of activities will ensure that despite this personalisation of each interview, the research aims are achieved in a consistent way across the sample. Figure 7.1 provides an example of how the portfolio of activities could be designed to enable consistency. In the example given, each research aim has three options of activities that could be adopted during the interview to achieve the research aim. It therefore does not matter which activity is chosen by the child, since the research aim will still be achieved and data gathered on that specific area. This method therefore permits the researcher to personalise each interview according to the interests and preferences of the child, while maintaining a level of consistency across the sample. This aligns with Prior's (2016) notion of bespoke and flexible interview tools.

Research aim	Activity
To explore the child's immediate family relationships	Building blocks used to depict and describe the members of the child's close family (see Figure 7.2). Probing questions as part of discussion used to investigate the nature of these relationships.
	Child draws a picture of their family, during which questions seek further information about the nature of the family relationships.
	Child is shown pictures on an iPad of different families. Discuss how the pictures are similar/different to the child's family. As part of discussion, probe to find out more about the nature of the child's own family relationships.
To explore the child's social experience in the school setting	Child draws their school (or class or playground if they prefer), during which discussion occurs about who they play with, how they feel in school, what they like and don't like, etc.
	An iPad is programmed with a quiz so that each screen displays a visual question prompt (question could also be on screen). The child answers verbally. A toy microphone could be included to make it fun, so that the child gets to say their answers into the microphone.
	Questions include: What is your favourite thing about school? Is there anything you don't like about school? Who do you sit by? Who do you play with? What happens at playtime?
	A 'scene' box is provided to the child containing figures and various props (see Figure 7.3). Ask them to recreate their school using these props, and to role-play what happens at school. Prompt the child to depict various social occasions and probe as to how the toy person feels at that time, etc.

Figure 7.1 An example of designing an activity portfolio

In order to keep the child's focus, it is good for all of the resources to be out of sight of the child, particularly at the start of the interview, and only revealed at the appropriate time. For example, a large treasure chest or brightly coloured box could be used to carry all of the resources into the interview setting. This serves to capture the interest of the child, and also to store the resources during the interview, so that the researcher can reach in and get out the relevant props at an appropriate time. It also gives the researcher the ability to keep up the pace of the interview, as they can put resources away and get new ones out when they have gained sufficient information from the child. Clearly, this needs to be done with sensitivity so as not to cause upset in the child, which again draws upon the researcher's early childhood expertise and experience.

Figure 7.2 Children using wooden blocks to depict their home

INDIVIDUAL/GROUP TASK

What experience have you had of communicating with young children in a sensitive manner? How can you ensure that you are attentive to the needs of the individual child during the interview, while also achieving the aims of your research?

Interview activities

Participatory approaches are valued in early childhood practice but are equally useful in academic research (O'Kane, 2001), so that frequently used educational resources and activities can be adapted for use in research contexts. This means that these objects and activities are readily familiar to the child, ensuring that the interview is relevant to the child's experience (Prior, 2016). Items such as Play-Doh, building blocks, drawing materials and Lego are valuable because the child can use these objects to depict their response in an open and unrestricted

Figure 7.3 Children using scenery and characters to retell a story to the researcher

way, and help to reveal the child's inner mind (Greig and Taylor, 2013). Visual resources such as books, pictures, magazines or vignettes (illustrating a scene, episode or scenario) on an iPad are useful as a prompt for discussion with the child (Scott, 2001). These resources could be highly specific (e.g. a book about bullying in order to facilitate discussion with the child on this topic) or they could be more general (e.g. a book about friendship), and the interviewer would gauge whether or not the child raises the notion of bullying within that. Small figurines, puppets, drama or role-play activities are beneficial at allowing the child to convey their ideas through non-verbal means. Such tools also allow the child to depersonalise their response (e.g. telling the researcher about any experiences of bullying that the puppet may have had), which seems to allow the child greater freedom of expression than if they were asked to explain any personal experiences (see Figure 7.5). Reality boxes could also be useful for exploring a child's inner feelings and ideas (Winter, 2016). Other items such as craft activities, bubbles, candles and music are helpful for children who find it difficult to engage in more structured tasks. They could freely play with these items while the researcher seeks to discuss issues pertinent to the research aims. In such a case, the play activities would serve to relax the child and facilitate them in responding freely. Children could also be asked creative questions amidst these activities, such as: 'If you could have three wishes, what would they be?' 'If you could take five photos of things that are precious to you, what would they be?' 'Describe to me what you would do in a perfect day, if you could choose whatever you wanted'. Scenarios can also be used to enable the child to relate easily to their everyday life (McCreery, 1996).

A significant benefit of play-based interviews is that they do not simply trigger impersonal 'learned' responses, but instead access the child's personal experience (Hay and Nye, 1998: 92). When children are enabled to describe their own reality and feelings, rather than being limited by answering preset questions, this provides more reliable responses. This also removes any confusion that young children often encounter, perhaps finding it difficult to distinguish between what is said and what is meant (Scott, 2001). Therefore, rather than providing children with preset categories or rigid questions, respondents can be

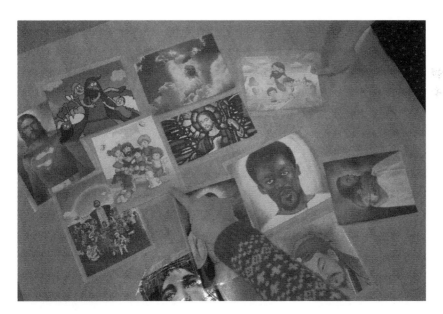

Figure 7.4 Children explaining which pictures they think most closely represent Jesus

enabled to use their own terminology to describe their family relationships, things they value and their personal experiences (Scott, 2001). This also contributes to the child feeling relaxed and at ease. Children tend to behave more naturally if they are less aware that they are being studied (Soto and Swadener, 2005), so the tone of the interview session should feel more like play than a staged research setting, and therefore provide more genuine and accurate observations of their thoughts, feelings, behaviours and ideas. To this end, note-taking should be avoided during the interview, and instead make use of video recording (if you have been ethically approved to do this by your university and the setting). To further reinforce the relaxed atmosphere, it is good practice to leave space for comfortable silences to allow participants time to think before responding (Prior, 2016).

During the play-based activities, the researcher needs to direct the conversation in order to observe or listen to precise aspects according to the research aims. While verbal exchanges are an element of play-based interviews, they are not the only means of gathering data. The child's facial expressions, body language, attitudes, overall

Figure 7.5 A researcher using a puppet to explore feelings with the child

willingness and interest, and non-verbal responses are of high value in effectively capturing the young child's authentic responses and behaviour, and must also be documented since they contribute to the depth of research findings facilitated by this method. For this reason, it is best to record the play-based interviews with a digital camcorder or similar. Watching the recording after the interview reveals a wealth of observation that may have been unnoticed by the researcher during the interview, as their attention was taken elsewhere. Examples of this may be a child sighing deeply every time school is mentioned, sombre body language during conversations about school playtimes, or a disinterest shown non-verbally in their reaction to books. These non-verbal observations are highly valuable and should be recorded as part of the research findings, hence the preference for video recording, although ethical consideration according to the research setting and university's ethics committee must be considered and adhered to strictly in this regard. Recording devices can be obtrusive and may make the child hesitant to talk freely (Graue and Walsh, 1998), so it is important to place the device as unobtrusively as possible (e.g. in a corner or behind a table), and not touch or refer to it for the remainder of the interview. The interview activities may also be used to distract the child from the fact that they are being recorded. As analysis commences, the interview may be documented using a transcription grid similar to Figure 7.6 in order to capture the wealth of data in a consistent and methodical manner. This example shows that not every single word requires transcribing, but only the key components that are relevant to the research aims. Both verbal and non-verbal responses should be documented fully. The information in the transcription grids may then be analysed using thematic analysis, and key themes compared across the sample.

INDIVIDUAL/GROUP TASK

How will you record/document your data? How can this be done with sensitivity to the participants? What ethical issues do you need to consider for your research project?

Child	Activity chosen	Verbal and non-verbal findings/observations
Research aim: To explore the child's immediate family relationships		
A, boy, age 5	Building blocks	Blocks: Child + Mum+ Dad + two brothers Child placed 'Dad' block far away from other family members, explaining that he was always at work: 'Dad cares more about his work than he does about us at home'. Explained Mum always busy, very stressed, always shouting at the kids: 'But I know she loves me. I just wish she had time for me sometimes'.
B, girl, age 4	iPad picture	Blocks: Child + Mum + Dad + dog Child stated that picture of family hugging and smiling was similar to hers. Spoke of happy times and memories. Body language relaxed and content as she spoke of family. Child said that picture of large extended family was not like his. Spoke of death of grandparent this year and missed them: 'I would like to have a sister so we can be best friends at home'. However, was very matter of fact and did not seem overly bothered about that.
Research aim: To explore the child's social experience in the school setting		
A	Scene box	Arriving at school: In classroom: . . . Lunchtime: . . . Home time: . . .

Figure 7.6 Example of a transcription grid

Practical considerations

It is good practice to carry out a small number of pilot interviews to test the interview activities. This is for the purpose of both ensuring that the participants understand and can engage with the activities, but also to ensure that the activities are meeting the requirements of the research aims. At this stage, any problems may be identified, in terms of comprehension or ambiguity, boredom or disinterest of the children, and any discrepancies between the child's understanding and researcher's intent (Scott, 2001). Necessary adaptations can then be made to the techniques following this pretest prior to continuing with the remainder of the sample.

It is important to make contact with the interview participants and their gatekeepers (the person who controls access to participants) in an appropriate manner. This may occur via telephone conversations, letter, email, or information sheets for both parent and child in advance of the interview. As part of this contact, you will need to communicate the essence of a play-based interview, which is important since adults and children alike may be nervous and hesitant about being interviewed. Adults may be particularly anxious about how the child may 'perform' and whether they will 'do as they are told' or 'say the wrong thing'. Explaining briefly about the notion of a play-based interview and the relaxed and informal nature will hopefully dispel most of these concerns. As a researcher entering the participant's world, it is also key to establish parameters before the interview begins, and it is best practice for the researcher to also reiterate these at the commencement of the interview. This may include the location of the interview, the presence of an adult for safeguarding purposes, the adult allowing the child freedom to respond without interruption or prompting, the atmosphere in which the child is able to say anything that they like and it won't be deemed offensive to the researcher, and the opportunity for the participants to withdraw at any time. If the researcher is previously unknown to the respondents, trust and openness must be built quickly at the beginning of the interview. This may be reflected in the choice of interview activities, which may include icebreaker-type activities to build rapport between researcher and child, alongside possibly attending the session prior to data gathering in order to facilitate familiarity of the researcher with the children (Prior, 2016). In addition, it may be beneficial for the researcher to attend the setting prior to data collection so that they are familiar to the children at the time of the interview.

The needs of the child are an essential consideration in research of this nature. Researchers need to be mindful that some topics may be of a sensitive nature for the children, and they may feel cautious when talking about matters such as family relationships, spirituality, bullying or personal feelings in front of others (Hay and Nye, 1998; Winter, 2016). The nature of the play-based interviews is designed to negate this and foster a sense of openness, and allow the child to talk freely and easily. However, it is important that ethical issues, such as informed consent, power relations, confidentiality, anonymity and the right to withdraw, are all fully considered during the design stage and implementation of any such research projects. It is also important that researchers are aware of appropriate sources of support to which they may signpost participants if the need arises.

An example project: exploring children's religious experience

Sixty-seven children aged 3 to 9 were interviewed using this play-based research method as part of doctoral research. The project was investigating religious activity in the family context. It was an ideal approach for this topic since it permitted the children to express to the researcher their experiences and perceptions about concepts and ideas that were potentially very difficult to verbalise. The research questions were how parental religious beliefs and activity impacted the child's religious experience; what specific religious activities in the family context were impacting them most; and whether age, gender or church affiliation impacted this in any way. Following initial icebreaker activities, the researcher asked the child to make a house and then their family using the building blocks. Once completed, the child was asked whether any of the bricks could be God and where they would place the 'God' brick in relation to them and their family. It was fascinating to explore which brick the child chose to represent God and why. For some children, the shape or colour was significant. For others, the size was important, so that some children built a tower to represent God rather than one single brick. Some children placed God right in the centre of their family, while others placed their brick high in the sky or far away from their house. This enabled the researcher to discuss the reasons for this with the child, in an appropriate way. (*Note*: Families opted to be part of this research knowing that it was about religious experience, so the researcher knew that the concept of 'God' was familiar to the children in some way.)

Other activities that were used to explore this topic included a scenery box with figures (whereby the child was asked to act out their experience of attending church), a puppet that was used to explore the child's understanding and perception of prayer, looking through Bible stories together to gauge the child's awareness and response to them, and a range of pictures of God on the iPad to discover which the child perceived to be most like God. All of these activities facilitated discussion with the child to an age-appropriate level and produced very illuminating findings, which observing parents also found interesting since many expressed that they didn't know their child could understand or perceive things such as this until they were older. For example, many children spoke of awareness of God's presence and the significance of this to them at difficult times. Some children expressed a developed understanding of God's forgiveness, which surprised their parents. Many of the children displayed similar attitudes to their parents regarding religion, whether cynical, ambivalent or deeply committed.

Strengths of play-based interviews

- The researcher was able to investigate children's religious experience in a targeted and specific manner.

- The researcher's early childhood expertise ensured that the interview activities were personalised for each child, while maintaining a consistent structure across the sample.

- The interviews were carried out successfully with both individual children and sibling groups.

- The interviews took place in a location familiar to the child.

- In-depth and insightful data were obtained.

Limitations of play-based interviews

- It required pre-existing early childhood skills and expertise of the researcher, in addition to knowledge of religious experience in children.

- Substantial resources were needed at each interview.

- A video recorder was used to record the interviews (in conjunction with university ethical approval to video-record).

- The researcher needed to be attentive and flexible to the child's interests and preferences.

- It was time-consuming, particularly in gaining ethical approval and the time needed to develop relationships with the setting and the children.

- It was necessary to carefully plan the process for handling sensitive information that may arise within the interviews.

Recommendations for future use

It is possible to adapt this research tool for use in a wide variety of research projects. Some possibilities are:

■ exploration of a particular aspect of a young child's life experience in the home or school setting;

■ a child's feelings or ideas could be examined in different contexts, so as to uncover whether their attitudes alter in different settings;

■ insight into a child's awareness of gender roles or cultural differences, perception of and response to children with disabilities or SEN, sibling relationships, friendship groups or family dynamics;

■ investigation of religious beliefs, understandings and experiences of the child; and

■ research into a child's attitudes, mindset and responses to learning.

Summary

■ Play-based interview techniques can facilitate children to reveal their thoughts, feelings and ideas without the constraints of language limitations, facilitating the child to feel relaxed and comfortable to converse about a range of topics.

■ These techniques require considerable thought, planning and existing early childhood expertise.

■ The approach can be used in a range of settings, with either individual children or small groups.

■ It permits semi-naturalistic observation.

■ Observations from the play-based interview can be recorded methodically for later analysis through a range of techniques, and can be used in isolation or as part of a wider project employing other methods and tools.

Recommended reading

Nolan, A., Macfarlane, K. and Cartmel, J. (2013) Moving along qualitative methodological pathways. In *Research in Early Childhood*. London: Sage, pp. 88–112.

O'Kane, C. (2008) The development of participatory techniques. In P. Christensen and A. James (eds), *Research with Children: Perspectives and Practices*. London: Routledge, pp. 125–155.

Roberts, H. (2008) Listening to children and hearing them. In P. Christensen and A. James (eds), *Research with Children*. London: Routledge, pp. 260–275.

Winter, K. (2016) Novel and creative qualitative methodologies with children. In J. Prior and J. Herwegen (eds), *Practical Research with Children*. New York: Routledge, pp. 166–187.

References

Bunge, M.J. (2006) The child, religion and the academy: developing robust theological and religious understandings of children and childhood. *The Journal of Religion*, 86(4): 549–579.

Clark, A., Flewitt, R., Hammersley, M. and Robb, M. (2013) *Understanding Research with Children and Young People*. London: Sage.

Donaldson, M. (1978) *Children's Minds*. London: HarperCollins.

Graue, M.E. and Walsh, D.J. (1998) *Studying Children in Context: Theories, Methods, and Ethics*. London: Sage.

Greig, A. and Taylor, J. (1999) *Doing Research with Children*. London: Sage.

Greig, A., Taylor, J. and MacKay, T. (2013) *Doing Research with Children*. London: Sage.

Hay, D. and Nye, R. (1998) *The Spirit of the Child*. London: Jessica Kingsley.

Mayall, B. (2001) Conversations with children: working with generational issues. In P. Christensen and A. James (eds), *Research with Children: Perspectives and Practices*. London: Routledge, pp. 120–135.

McCreery, E. (1996) Talking to young children about things spiritual. In R. Best (ed.), *Education, Spirituality and the Whole Child*. London: Cassell, pp. 196–205.

O'Kane, C. (2001) The development of participatory techniques: facilitating children's views about decisions which affect them. In P. Christensen and A. James (eds), *Research with Children: Perspectives and Practices*. London: Routledge, pp. 136–159.

O'Kane, C. (2008) The development of participatory techniques. In P. Christensen and A. James (eds), *Research with Children: Perspectives and Practices*. London: Routledge, pp. 125–155.

Piaget, J. (1967) *Six Psychological Studies*. London: University of London Press.

Prior, J. (2016) The use of semi-structured interviews with young children. In J. Prior and J. Herwegen (eds), *Practical Research with Children*. New York: Routledge, pp. 109–126.

Quinn, S.F. (2014) The organisation of memory and thought. In S. Robson and S.F. Quinn (eds), *The Routledge International Handbook of Young Children's Thinking and Understanding*. London: Routledge, pp. 54–64.

Scott, J. (2001) Children as respondents: the challenge for quantitative methods. In P. Christensen and A. James (eds), *Research with Children: Perspectives and Practices*. London: Routledge, pp. 98–119.

Soto, L. and Swadener, B. (2005) *Power and Voice in Research*. New York: Peter Lang.

Winter, K. (2016) Novel and creative qualitative methodologies with children. In J. Prior and J. Herwegen (eds), *Practical Research with Children*. New York: Routledge, pp. 166–187.

8 Using the mosaic approach as an ethnographic methodology

Zenna Kingdon

Introduction

In this chapter, I intend to demonstrate the way in which the mosaic approach (Clark and Moss, 2001) can be used not simply as a method, but as a methodology (in this context, a way of thinking about research). An overview of the way in which the method was developed and initially used is discussed. I will establish how the approach is situated paradigmatically and its relationship to ethnography as a methodology. Ethnographic research necessitates moving into the world of the subject. The studies are usually situated within the natural setting of communities and cultures, and involve observations that are comprehensive, in depth and conducted longitudinally.

In this chapter, I demonstrate how I have utilised the mosaic approach as an ethnographic methodology. By immersing myself in the setting, drawing on critical reflection and layering the mosaics, I have developed an innovative approach that extends the initial approach developed by Clark and Moss (2001).

The mosaic approach

With an increased interest in participative research with children, particularly young children, there has been an increase in interest in appropriate tools for data generation (Harcourt et al., 2011). Methods that are suggested to be particularly suitable for use with younger children include: drawing, photography, observations, semi-structured interviews, child conferencing, setting tours, and videos (Clark, 2005; Cook and Hess, 2007; Einarsdottir, 2005).

Clark and Moss (2001) created what they called the mosaic approach, which is also referred to as a 'framework for listening' (p. 5). The approach is grounded in a perspective that 'acknowledges children and adults as co-constructors of meaning' (p. 1). The mosaic is a multisensory approach that allows the researcher to gather a clear picture of the child's perspective or view of their experiences within a setting. Clark and Moss (2001) developed this approach to work with very young children; it was initially intended for use with children under 5, and has been used extensively with 3-year-olds as well as children under 2 (Clark, 2005). They developed several data collection methods, and advocate that not all need to be utilised to create a mosaic. To gather the necessary information, the researcher engages with the child in a number of activities within the setting. These can include: a map of the setting; photographs of the setting taken by the child; drawings of the setting or people within it; key person interviews or conferences; child conferencing; observations; parent interviews; tours; and audio or videotapes of the setting.

Clark and Moss (2001) demonstrate that whilst not all the activities need to be undertaken to complete a mosaic, a number of them must be utilised in order that the child has the best opportunity to demonstrate his or her opinion and in order that there are sufficient data from which conclusions can be drawn. The researcher then brings together the different pieces of the mosaic to provide a holistic view of the child's experiences and voice.

When Clark and Moss (2001) began their work, the children were offered disposable cameras. Such an approach meant that there were limitations; the researcher told the children that they needed to think very carefully before using the camera because they were often limited to only 12 pictures (Rogers and Evans, 2008). More recent research has utilised digital cameras or a combination of digital and disposable ones (Einarsdottir, 2005). In many research projects where children are given digital cameras, adults are with them when the photographs are taken. Where they are given disposable cameras, they can be alone with the camera. Researchers, including Clark and Moss (2001), Einarsdottir (2005) and Rogers and Evans (2008), all found that when the children were enabled to be alone with the camera, they took a greater number of photographs and photographed items and areas that would not necessarily be approved of by adults, such as the toilets and areas of the outside space where they are not supposed to play.

The mosaic approach argues for children as co-researchers, and in my research this is how the children are positioned – they are able to explore aspects of their experiences in ways that they find engaging and meaningful for them.

Usually, the mosaic is developed in one piece, as shown in Figure 8.1.

INDIVIDUAL/GROUP TASK

Read *Listening to Children: The Mosaic Approach* (Clark and Moss, 2001) in order to understand fully the approach. Why is hearing the voice of the child important?

Gaby	Observation	Conferencing	Cameras	Tours	Maps	Parents	Practitioner
Friends and role play with friends	♦	♦	♦	♦	♦	♦	♦
Adults being there							♦
Making things		♦	♦	♦			
Singing		♦	♦	♦	♦	♦	
Tasty food		♦				♦	
Wish to join in with 4-year-olds				♦	♦	♦	

Figure 8.1 Mosaic example

Paradigm and perspective: who am I as a researcher?

When undertaking any research project, we must first acknowledge who we are as researchers, what influences our thinking and how our beliefs frame our research; only by understanding this can we then consider which paradigm will frame our research. The term paradigm is a philosophical term that refers to a school of thought or a set of values or beliefs (Ma, 2016). It is unusual for researchers to define their work in terms of the paradigm; usually, they tend to acknowledge whether they are adhering to quantitative or qualitative data collection methods (Cohen et al., 2017).

A paradigm can be considered to be a basic set of beliefs that guide action, or 'a set of propositions that explain how the world is perceived' (Sarantakos, 2005: 30). There are generally regarded to be three paradigms: positivism; post- or anti-positivism, usually referred to as interpretivist; and finally critical theory. Each paradigm will provide the framework for the methodologies employed by the researcher. Therefore, the paradigm that a researcher utilises will be underpinned by their values.

Interpretive researchers do not believe in universal truths about the nature of humanity. Instead, they recognise that individuals construe reality differently from one another; the nature of the research 'is about realities and relationships' (Sarantakos, 2005: 37). Constructions of reality include 'making accounts of the world around us and gaining impressions based on culturally defined and historically situated interpretations and personal experiences' (Sarantakos, 2005: 37). Interpretive researchers likewise recognise that the observer makes a difference to the observed and that reality is constructed.

The third paradigm, critical theory, is said to have been developed in the Frankfurt School. It assesses the relationship between theory and practice in the social sciences. The theorists looked back at the work of Aristotle (1925) in the first instance, and his concern with praxis or action. Aristotle (1925) did not view elements of the arts, including ethics, politics and education, as rigorous sciences. Fundamentally, the paradigm of critical theory supports social emancipation; it assists individuals in understanding how their aims and purposes are distorted and suppressed, and the types of actions needed to liberate them.

Much of my research is concerned with considering the ways in which reality is shaped by social, political, cultural, economic and gendered values and experiences. I am concerned with seeking and understanding the views of young children in order to better understand the experiences of their lives; the mosaic approach allows me to do this. While my work draws on aspects of critical theory, it cannot be truly identified as such, and therefore it can be seen to be situated within an interpretivist paradigm. The interpretivist paradigm is concerned with understanding the subjective world of human experience, and is reliant on thick descriptions to illustrate the complexity of situations and to share experiences (Cohen et al., 2017). The multi-method approach of the mosaic approach supports my interpretive approach.

INDIVIDUAL/GROUP TASK

Think about your own values and what has influenced you. Consider how these may influence you as a researcher. What approach to research do you want to take?

Ethnographic research

Ethnography is the study of culture and behaviour; it is 'a portrayal and explanation of social groups and situations in their real-life contexts' (Cohen et al., 2017: 292). Ethnography is concerned with the researcher developing a relationship with the social actors, engaging in their environment, observations and descriptions of social action, with the researcher engaging in everyday experiences of the social actors and learning to understand their experiences (Gobo and Marciniak, 2016). Ethnography usually involves participant observation among other methods of data collection, and is situated in qualitative methodologies (Siraj-Blatchford and Siraj-Blatchford, 2001).

Ethnographic studies are interpretative; they aim to 'provide a holistic account that includes the views, perspectives, beliefs, intentions and values of the subjects of the study' (Siraj-Blatchford and Siraj-Blatchford, 2001: 194). Ethnographic studies have been used by early childhood researchers for a range of purposes, and specifically to gain an understanding of children's experiences in particular settings and when researching play. Ethnography can 'paint in the fine-grained reality of educational processes within early childhood settings' (Siraj-Blatchford and Siraj-Blatchford, 2001: 194). The data for ethnographic research are usually gathered using a range of different sources, with observation and informal conversations being seen as key.

The mosaic approach (Clark and Moss, 2001) could be argued to be an ethnographic methodology. It provides appropriate tools, including observations, interviews and documentation, for such ethnographic research, and is underpinned by a paradigmatic approach that is concerned with giving voice to the child.

INDIVIDUAL/GROUP TASK

Consider what it is that you intend to gain from the research. Are you in a setting where you could carry out ethnographic research? Ethnographic research takes time. Do you have the time to immerse yourself in a setting in order that you can carry out ethnographic research?

Utilising the mosaic approach and adapting it for ethnographic research

The mosaic approach (Clark and Moss, 2001) was developed in order that researchers could gain an understanding of individual children's experiences within their early childhood settings. In order to utilise the mosaic approach, researchers had to develop a relationship with the child and engage in their environment, and hence the ethnographic nature of the research.

I have used the mosaic approach to conduct two significant pieces of research, both of which were concerned with children's experiences of play, and in particular role play. Both pieces of research could be considered to utilise an ethnographic methodology, and I have adapted the mosaic approach. In the first instance, I collected data with 5- and 6-year-old children, and in the second I utilised an ethnographic approach over an extended period of time working with 3- and 4-year-old children.

Study 1: role play in Year 1

The first study considered Year 1 children's experiences of role play in their classroom. The research was conducted in two rural schools in which the Year 1 children were within mixed-year classes. In the first school, Moortown Primary (all names are anonymised), the children were in a Foundation and Year 1 class, while in St Mary's Primary the children were in a mixed Year 1 and Year 2 class. Children in Year 1 were offered the opportunity to participate (see Chapter 2, this volume). The differing mix of year groups allowed for a further comparison of the children's experiences of role play within their setting.

In this piece of research, six tools were used: observation, role play, photographs, maps, drawings, and child conferences or interviews, all of which are methods utilised by Clark and Moss (2001). I conducted observations of all of the children on each of my visits. I identified role-play activities in which the children participated in each class (these did not necessarily occur in the identified role-play area in each classroom). I spent time in the classroom getting to know the children and observing them while they were engaged in their chosen activities. The children were informed that I would be revisiting them in a week's time. Children were given a camera and asked to take photographs of their role play and play that they enjoyed over that period. The use of cameras allowed for immersion in their setting, an approach associated with ethnography (Needham, 2016). They were also asked to make maps of their learning areas and areas in which they enjoyed playing within their school (see Figure 8.2). I made it clear that it was possible that the two areas could be one and the same. On returning, I looked at the maps and the photographs with the children who were willing to share them and discuss them; this became a conference activity, as described by Clark and Moss (2001). The final activity of drawings and child conferences were completed together.

The immersive nature of the data provided for an ethnographic approach in which mosaics could be generated. From the mosaics, themes were identified to be explored. While the two cohorts of children were in differently constituted classes, their experiences, while slightly more formal in St Mary's Primary, were similar.

Figure 8.2 A map of learning and playing areas drawn by a child in St Mary's Primary School

The responses to the child conferences were comparable: outdoor play was discussed by every child, and likewise friendships were of importance to all the children.

Study 2: role play in packaway settings

In this project, I used the mosaic approach (Clark and Moss, 2001) to understand children's experiences of role play in packaway early childhood education and care settings. The data were generated over an extended period of time utilising an ethnographic approach, in two settings, Home-Fell Nursery and All Hallows Preschool. In total, eight children, their key persons, their parents and two setting managers participated in this research project – four children in each setting. In both settings, I spent time getting to know the children and establishing a relationship with them before I began any research.

Data were generated in a range of ways. These included observations, participative and non-participative and snapshot, conferencing activites with children, parents and key persons, children's photographs, drawings and maps, and informal discussions with setting managers. Observations of the children and their photographs were essential in generating data and were the starting point with the other activities, including conferences building on the initial data.

Three iterations of each child's mosaic were created. The first was created once I had completed my data generation and collection with the child. This formed the first layer of the three-dimensional mosaic. I then conducted a conference with the child's key person, as per Clark and Moss (2001), using a semi-structured interview schedule. At the end of the conference, I showed the key person the first layer of the mosaic and asked them to tell me what they felt I had missed. I only showed them the mosaic once they had completed their semi-structured interview in order that they were able to provide their own reflections without influences from the previous mosaic. The information they then gave was added to create the second layer of the mosaic. Finally, I conducted a conference with the child's parent using a semi-structured interview schedule. When I finished the parent conference, I showed them the second version of the mosaic and asked them what the key person and I had failed to observe. The information that they gave provided the third layer of the mosaic. In every instance, there were interests added by the key person and further ones added by the parent, enabling me to develop a more rounded understanding of the child. Critical reflection was essential in developing the three-dimensional mosaics. The layering allowed for thick descriptions of the children's experiences and for critical reflection on the data (Cohen et al., 2017).

Each morning on arrival at a setting, I would draw a plan of the way in which the room had been set up for that day (see Figure 8.3). It seemed important to know where everything was; it also meant that when I followed children around the setting, it was possible to discuss where they started and where they went, demonstrating that they did not necessarily use the space in the way in which the practitioners intended.

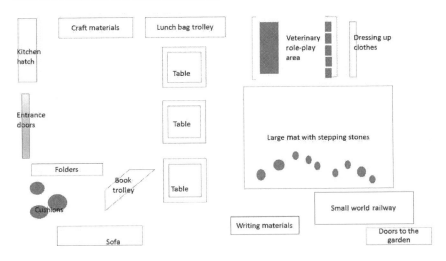

Figure 8.3 The set-up at All Hallows Preschool on one day

From the data, a number of themes emerged. These included:

- the use of multiple play sites for role-play activities;

- children's demonstration of positive self-esteem and effective social behaviours;

- the role of the practitioners specifically concerning the organisation in packaway settings; and

- the role of the adult as creator and facilitator of role play.

Additionally, a series of photographs taken by all of the children led to my recognition that as adults, we often make assumptions based on our ideas about what children are trying to say or share with us. This area of interest for children had gone unnoticed both by me as the researcher but also by the practitioners who worked with them. As adults, we sometimes misinterpret children's work or their intentions. An extended example of this was the children's deliberate photographs of feet, usually their own but sometimes other people's. Discussions of these photographs demonstrated their importance to the children, while I had previously dismissed them as misfires of the camera.

These two projects were concerned with hearing the voice of the child. They were made possible by utilising the mosaic approach (Clark and

Moss, 2001). In each instance, a range of tools were employed. In utilising the mosaic approach, I felt that I was utilising research tools that were tried and tested. The second project, role play in packaway settings, was conducted over an extended period of time and moved the mosaic approach from a method, a way of collecting data, to an ethnographic methodology in which I was immersed in the setting and was able to understand the lived experiences of the children. Using the mosaic approach helped me to understand children's experience of play and role play.

Strengths and limitations of using the mosaic approach as an ethnographic methodology

Strengths

The mosaic approach is an appropriate, holistic tool that enables researchers to work with children and practitioners to generate data that hears the voice of the child. It utilises an approach that provides a rich description of the child while endorsing a view of children as stakeholders with rights (Clark, 2005). The 1989 United Nations Convention on the Rights of the Child (UNCRC) brought about a challenge to the dominant discourse of children as objects of research, and began to recognise children as competent social actors who could comment effectively on their experiences and perspectives (Dockett et al., 2011; Smith, 2011). It has led to an expansion of research that attempts to listen to the voice of the child and 'a new culture in relation to children's rights and interests' (Smith, 2011: 12):

- The mosaic approach enabled me to listen to the voice of the child, to understand what was important to them and to discover what they think about issues that affect them.

- In both projects, the children were particularly keen on using the cameras and taking photographs of things that were important to them or to their friends.

- The children were 'active research participants . . . competent contributors of valid opinions' (Harcourt and Conroy, 2011: 39). The children generated data that I had not anticipated, nor conceived would be important to them.

Researchers who are committed to working with children are expected to position children positively, seeing them as reliable witnesses in reporting on their own lives. The mosaic approach enables them to do so.

Limitations

The mosaic approach is not without challenge:

- I needed to develop a relationship with the child and engage in their environment, all of which can be time-consuming.

- Participative research with children, particularly young children, is reliant on appropriate tools for data generation (Harcourt et al., 2011). In my second project, the children all appeared to find the concept of map-making challenging.

- As a researcher, it is often difficult not to have expectations of what children will do in certain circumstances. My views were challenged particularly when the children were drawing while participating in a conference activity.

- While not all the activities need to be undertaken to complete a mosaic, a number of them must be utilised in order that the child has the best opportunity to demonstrate his or her opinion; likewise, this can be time-consuming.

- The activities need to make the children feel 'empowered and enabled' (Harcourt et al., 2011: 73). Therefore, it is essential that the methods are appropriate and engaging, and consider the age and the needs of the children.

Including children as genuine participants of research remains a challenge, and research projects must be created with consideration of the children's needs from design to dissemination (Te One, 2011). The mosaic approach places the child at the centre of the research, and therefore allows their voice to be heard.

Summary

In this chapter, I set out to demonstrate the mosaic approach (Clark and Moss, 2001) and to determine the ways in which it could be adapted to move beyond being simply a method to a methodology, and specifically an ethnography methodology:

- The approach was designed in order to listen to children, to give them voice and to aid researchers in understanding their lived experiences.

- Research is always framed by the paradigmatic view of the researcher.

- Those of us working within the interpretivist paradigm or within the field of critical theory are concerned by the experiences of the individual. At the same time, we are aware that research participants are affected by family and friends, as well as cultural, social, political, economic and gendered values and experiences.

- The mosaic approach provides a range of tools that allow the researcher to develop a holistic view of the child.

- Multiple tools are always used in order that sufficient data are collected to draw conclusions.

- The tools used have been tried by a number of researchers and found to be effective, particularly when working with young children (Clark, 2005; Cook and Hess, 2007; Einarsdottir, 2005; Rogers and Evans, 2008).

- The mosaic approach can be used as an ethnographic methodology when its methods are implemented over an extended period of time.

Recommended reading

Clark, A. (2005) Listening to and involving young children: a review of research and practice. *Early Child Development and Care*, 175(6): 489–505.

Clark, A. and Moss, P. (2001) *Listening to Children: The Mosaic Approach*. London: Joseph Rowntree Foundation.

Einarsdottir, J. (2005) Playschool in pictures: children's photographs as a research method. *Early Child Development and Care*, 175(6): 523–541.

Harcourt, D. Perry, B. and Waller, T. (2011) *Researching Young Children's Perspectives: Debating the Ethics and Dilemmas of Educational Research with Children*. London: Routledge.

References

Aristotle (1925) *The Nicomachean Ethics*. Oxford: Oxford University Press.

Clark, A. (2005) Listening to and involving young children: a review of research and practice. *Early Child Development and Care*, 175(6): 489–505.

Clark, A. and Moss, P. (2001) *Listening to Children: The Mosaic Approach*. London: Joseph Rowntree Foundation.

Cohen, L., Manion, L. and Morrison, K. (2017) *Research Methods in Education*, 8th edn. London: Routledge.

Cook, T. and Hess, E. (2007) What the camera sees and from whose perspective: fun methodologies for engaging children in enlightening adults. *Childhood*, 14(29): 29–45.

Dockett, S., Einardottir, J. and Perry, B. (2011) Balancing methodologies and methods in researching with young children. In D. Harcourt, B. Perry and T. Waller (eds), *Researching Young Children's Perspectives*. London: Routledge, pp. 68–81.

Einarsdottir, J. (2005) Playschool in pictures: children's photographs as a research method. *Early Child Development and Care*, 175(6): 523–541.

Gobo, G. and Marciniak, L. (2016) What is ethnography? In D. Silverman (ed.), *Qualitative Research*, 4th edn. London: Sage, pp. 103–120.

Harcourt, D. and Conroy, H. (2011) Informed consent: processes and procedures seeking research partnership with children. In D. Harcourt, B. Perry and T. Waller (eds), *Researching Young Children's Perspectives: Debating the Ethics and Dilemmas of Educational Research with Children*. London: Routledge, pp. 38–51.

Harcourt, D. Perry, B. and Waller, T. (2011) *Researching Young Children's Perspectives: Debating the Ethics and Dilemmas of Educational Research with Children*. London: Routledge.

Ma, J. (2016) Making sense of research methodology. In I. Palaiologou, D. Needham and T. Male (eds), *Doing Research in Education Theory an d Practice*. London: Sage, pp. 18–36.

Needham, D. (2016) Constructing the hypotheses/creating the research question(s). In I. Palaiologou, D. Needham and T. Male (eds), *Doing Research in Education Theory and Practice*. London: Sage, pp. 59–79.

Rogers, S. and Evans, J. (2008) *Inside Role-Play in Early Childhood Education*. London: Routledge.

Sarantakos, S. (2005) *Social Research*, 3rd edn. Basingstoke: Palgrave Macmillan.

Siraj-Blatchford, I. and Siraj-Blatchford, J. (2001) An ethnographic approach to researching young children's learning. In G. MacNaughton, S. Rolfe and I. Siraj-Blatchford (eds), *Doing Early Childhood Research: International Perspectives on Theory and Practice*. Maidenhead: Open University Press, pp. 193–207.

Smith, A. (2011) Respecting children's rights and agency: theoretical insights into ethical research procedures. In D. Harcourt, B. Perry and T. Waller (eds), *Researching Young Children's Perspectives: Debating the Ethics and Dilemmas of Educational Research with Children*. London: Routledge, pp. 11–25.

Te One, S. (2011) Supporting children's participation rights: curriculum and research approaches. In D. Harcourt, B. Perry and T. Waller (eds), *Researching Young Children's Perspectives: Debating the Ethics and Dilemmas of Educational Research with Children*. London: Routledge, pp. 85–99.

Using video to research outdoors with young children

Gary Beauchamp, Chantelle Haughton, Cheryl Ellis, Siân Sarwar, Jacky Tyrie, Dylan Adams and Sandra Dumitrescu

This chapter will examine the positive and negative features of using video as a research tool with children in early childhood education and care. The chapter will be structured around, and will use examples from, the progress (from beginning to end) of a real, recent research project looking at young children's play in a woodland setting. In this project, some children wore digital video cameras (some built into glasses and some worn on a chest harness), which provided a unique child's view of their play and interactions, both with each other and the environment. We will examine the justification of the decision to use video as a research tool, the planning and implementation of the project, the analysis of data, and the subsequent dissemination of findings. It will conclude by identifying the unique contribution video can make to research methods, particularly outdoors, in early childhood.

Researching outdoor education with video

The benefits of outdoor learning, or learning outside of the classroom (LOtC), particularly in early education, have been widely reported (Davies and Hamilton, 2018) and outdoor learning is an explicit part of curricula and pedagogy in many countries. Within this research, there has been a specific focus on outdoor play, but there is a 'significant lacuna and, therefore, opportunity in the LOtC research field with respect to theorising and philosophising the methods and benefits of such pedagogy' (Hawxwell et al., 2018: 9) – echoing earlier calls for stronger empirical and conceptual understandings of learning in the outdoor classroom (e.g. Dillon et al., 2006; Rickinson et al., 2004). To help address this shortfall, a research project was developed as part of a small-scale community engagement project between a university and a local primary school. The project had a learning and teaching focus and involved children in the reception class (4–5 years) working and playing in a woodland setting.

Why use video as a research tool?

The decision to use video as a research tool in the project was based on the growing variety of its use in research (Schuck and Kearney, 2006), including video diaries (Jones et al., 2016), video-stimulated reflective dialogues (Adams and Beauchamp, 2018), synchronous (real-time) interviews at a distance (Deakin and Wakefield, 2014), asynchronous video sharing (Rowan et al., 2015) and adult–child interactions in the early childhood classroom (Fisher and Wood, 2012). Many studies use video as a research tool with adults, where issues such as ethics (see Chapter 2, this volume) are potentially more straightforward. With young children, however, although there are many positive and negative features of using video as a research tool, the situation is more complicated. The benefits of using video with young children are summed up by Cowan (2014), in that it provides 'a temporal and sequential record, offering information about an event as it unfolds moment-by-moment whilst preserving the simultaneity and synchrony of interaction' (p. 6).

The decision to use video was made very early in the project planning, for a mixture of pragmatic and research reasons. Pragmatically, video recording is a 'natural method' in that it does not require research training (Walker, 2012). Also, the children were to be given free play opportunities and it would be impossible to follow them with cameras. Therefore, the decision was made to ask them to wear cameras, either chest-mounted, or, more usefully, built into glasses frames that they were asked to wear. This also gave valuable data as particularly the glasses cameras allowed the research team to literally see what they were seeing, whereas the chest cameras did not move when they turned their head. This allows the researcher to follow features of interactions (both with other children and the environment), such as 'gaze, facial expression and movement – alongside talk and its features, which can be repeatedly re-viewed in different ways and in different contexts' (Cowan, 2014: 6). Although the aim was to limit the intrusion of the research as much as possible, both types of cameras presented some problems. Even though the chest cameras were small, they were slightly obtrusive and restricting due to the harness holding them in place – an example of the 'camera as distractor' (Leung and Hawkins, 2011). The camera glasses, even though they were only a frame with no lenses, were slightly too big for the small children, so stretchy headbands were developed to hold them in place. In addition, to start with, some children were very aware of the cameras and slightly self-conscious. By giving them the choice of what to wear and when, the children quickly lost this awareness, particularly when engaged in play. Although this meant some video data were lost as children chose to stop wearing the cameras, ethically they also maintained their voice in the research process. Both cameras recorded good-quality sound, and this was very useful in analysing speech and interactions.

Planning the project

Preliminary meetings were held by the research team to decide on the activities to be offered and the best way to collect research data during the project. This was essential as the research method would need to be clearly outlined in permission letters to all parties, in an age-appropriate format.

The project set-up involved:

- initial meetings with the head teacher, parents, children and whole school staff;

- planning with the teacher the project dates and practical realities of dates and timings, etc.;

■ risk-assessing the activities and site for the visits and activities pre-project and daily within the project;

■ gaining ethical approval through the university system;

■ gaining pupil, parental and school-informed consent; and

■ planning how the children and teachers would get to the woodland site on the university campus.

The pupils came in small groups of about 15 to the university campus woodland setting. A series of Forest School weekly sessions with the children and the teacher were run by the university team, supported by students and observed by the class teacher and other school staff. As well as videoing during the 'free play' or 'wild play' sessions at the end of each visit, which was the particular research focus for this project, the research team also observed and made field notes.

The main sources of data collection were very small, high-definition mobile video recorders carried by pupils, unobtrusively attached to them or their clothing so that recordings were eventually made unconsciously to try to capture 'naturalistic' data from children playing as they normally would. These cameras provided a unique child's view of their play and interactions, both with each other and the environment. There was an awareness, however, that as research methods become more innovative, they could potentially become more invasive into the comfort of children's worlds and play. This also has implications for ethics, which will be considered later in this chapter (see also Chapter 2, this volume).

Implementing the project

During the implementation phase of the project, the use of video presented the research team with both opportunities (as outlined above) and challenges. These challenges were technical, organisational and ethical.

Technical challenges

The immediate technical challenge of using video is ensuring that the cameras are all charged and have capacity to record the session – which means downloading video from the previous session, of which more later. With most cameras, we needed to add a memory card to ensure that they had sufficient capacity to hold the data (in other projects with video, we have had to have a card reader or laptop with one built in to download any data *in situ* if needed so they can be used again). As there were many cameras there was a large amount of data to download, but this could be done when the children had left at our convenience – although this did take a considerable period of time depending on the number of cameras. However, it became very important to clearly label each file (e.g. week 1, glasses camera 1 = W1GC1) and all files from one week kept in labelled folders. This was only possible if each camera was also labelled. If you wanted to track an individual child, it would also be necessary to keep a list of what camera they used each session.

We also faced considerable unexpected challenges in finding a secure, password-protected storage area for the data – as promised in the ethics application – that would also be of sufficient capacity (in this case, over 130 GB). This is even more important with General Data Protection Regulation (GDPR) regulations, so it is worth planning this a long way ahead of starting the project, and may even mean a cost for larger projects. Having established a secure storage area, in this case on the university servers, we then faced the challenge of all staff getting secure access to the files!

Organisational challenges

Besides ensuring all cameras were charged and had space on them to record, if more than one person is involved in the project, it is also important to decide who is going to do this and when. Also, you need to be clear where they will be stored, who will collect them and bring them back to the research setting, and who will put them on charge afterwards. It is worth checking if anyone else is going to use the cameras, and if so when, and remind them to take their data off the cameras – you will not be popular if you record over someone else's work. It is very important to download your work as soon as possible after the fieldwork, but you need to be clear who is doing this if more than one person is involved. Finally, when using video, either fixed or mobile cameras, they will need to be set up, or in our case attached to the children – not always an easy task when they know they are off to play in the woods. With fixed cameras, there is also the need to bring stands that fit the cameras (test this before you leave as bitter experience suggests that the last person to use them may have left part of the stand attached to another camera!) and possibly power extension leads.

Ethical challenges

As the video was a very important (if not the most important) data source, it was obviously desirable that the team gathered as much as possible. However, this brought about a potential tension between gathering data and giving the children a free choice to participate. In a reflective note after the session, one of the research team noted:

> We reminded the children each week that they could choose if they wanted to participate in the research and they could choose to wear the cameras or not. I felt that in the early weeks, they were excited to wear the equipment and there would be a 'camera queue' and 'waiting list'. The novelty soon wore off, but some children chose to wear the cameras consistently over the weeks. Some swapped between body cameras and glasses. Sometimes we tried to steer them to wear the same type of equipment as maybe this would help us in the research to have a similar approach to recording the data. There was some discussion about this within the research team, and I struggled with this as I felt we could tip the power balance.

This is one aspect of 'power', which also includes age, size and status, where 'power and status differentials raise the possibility that children may find it difficult to dissent, disagree or say things that adults may not like' (Punch and Oancea, 2014: 52).

In addition, the children were being offered the chance to have 'free' wild play, but at the same time there was the potential to gather potentially intrusive up-close observations of this play. Furthermore, as the children were playing in a woodland surrounded by roads and houses, there were inevitably boundaries and rules about its use. So, was the play actually free? This was one of several conflicting priorities between the needs of the children and the research. Another was the potential to freely explore the woodland versus safety. This is part of the risk/benefit equation that needs to be considered by researchers in relation to those involved in the project (both those being researched and researchers themselves), especially with young children. For example, besides the more obvious physical risk of harm, such as falling from a tree branch or slipping in the mud, we also need to reflect that 'risks of research on children can include psychological risks, ranging from a feeling of temporary worry to longer lasting emotional disturbance' (Coady, 2001: 68). All these factors need to be considered at the earliest stages of the research planning (which may, at one extreme, lead to the research not taking place) and also when ethical approval is sought for a research project, and even at the inception of the project – although the earlier consideration will make parts of the ethics application easier as you have already identified the risks involved.

INDIVIDUAL/GROUP TASK

Decide how you would research and record the risks, to the children and to the adults, when taking young children on a trip to a woodland setting. In early childhood settings, you may be able to ask for examples of risk assessments and policies to see how they undertake this exercise. Decide on how you would make a final decision to undertake the research project, balancing the benefits for children to take risks and their safety.

Generic research challenges

There were also more generic challenges, which are common to most types of research, particularly in educational settings or when working with practitioners. The first of these is the changing roles from 'practitioner' to 'researcher' during the research session – although this also applies when practitioners conduct research in their own classroom and pupils are not sure if they are teacher or researcher. In this instance, some of the research team helped in the first part of the session based on Forest School activities (practitioners). In the second 'free play' part of the session, they then became observers (researchers, taking field notes, etc.). As one member of the team wrote in a reflective note:

> Those of us involved in gathering data took a behind-the-scenes role in planning and implementation of the sessions, therefore

adopting a focused sustained 'researcher' role. It was interesting to see how the children quickly came to recognise this and were able to distinguish the different adult roles. For example, sometimes they discussed issues in the learning and teaching activities with the Forest School delivery team, but in contrast one child stopped at the log circle to ask me, '[name of researcher], are we going to do play and research today?'

To help alleviate this, Beauchamp and Haughton (2012) suggest that 'perhaps the first step in making the transition to researcher is to examine the *purpose* of your presence . . . Although it may seem slightly contrary, it may be easiest to consider first what you are *not* there to do' (p. 148, original emphasis). Furthermore, as Delamont (2002) points out, 'being useful in the setting is often attractive, but not always possible' (p. 155).

The analysis of data

In recent years, advances in technology and the widespread availability of high-quality video provide 'powerful ways of collecting, sharing, studying, presenting, and archiving detailed cases of practice' (Derry et al., 2010: 4). A key feature of video in analysis is that it provides a multimodal perspective, including a record of many different modes such as movement and posture, gesture, gaze, spoken language, facial expression, sound, proximity, the sound of voice, and movements. However, in analysing these semiotic modes, we need to be aware that the 'multimodal nature of communication is complex and layered' (Lacković, 2018: 3), particularly with young children.

INDIVIDUAL/GROUP TASK

Discuss the design of a recording sheet that could be used by a research team to use while watching video to record some or all of the following: movement, posture, gesture, gaze, spoken language, facial expression, sound, proximity to each other and adults, locations of activities and movements between them. This could involve maps (to mark locations and movements), tally charts, individual notes, etc.

Another advantage of using video in research is that when analysing data 'in comparison to field notes and interview transcripts, video data allows the researcher to go back and revisit "the field" through repeated viewings of the video' (Gylfe et al., 2016: 135). Also, when analysing data, the use of multiple cameras also allows multiple perspectives, which can provide additional context, such as when two children wearing cameras talk to each other, allowing the face of each to be seen instead of just one. This also presented some challenges in trying to coordinate the different videos. In hindsight, the team would have included a simple starting point, such as a simultaneous clap before the children went off to play, which would help align the videos to establish contemporaneous actions – even if widely separated in the woodland.

Another advantage of analysing video is that when a team of researchers view video together, 'they bring their own experiences and points of view to the setting and can share different interpretations of the events that unfold' (Van Es et al., 2014: 342). In the research team, there were many specialisms (such as music, play and early education), and each offered a different 'lens' to the analysis – although this also presented occasional challenges when the same episode (such as bouncing on a branch or hitting a tree with a stick) was perceived in different ways. As such, video can provide a tool for 'video reflection' (Tripp and Rich, 2012), not just on individual practice (such as reflections by teachers on video of their classroom teaching), but also on the interactions of others, without the need to be present at the time of the event – although the use of contemporaneous field notes from researchers present at the time was also useful in analysis.

As with all qualitative analysis, there are many options for interpreting and coding responses, depending on your ontological and epistemological stance. In this project, the team adopted an interpretative approach, with the themes emerging from the data. The video was watched by the whole team at the same time and themes/codes noted individually, before further refining as a group to establish agreed codes. However, given the sheer quantity of data in terms of watching in real time, it became necessary to allocate different researchers to different videos in their own time. This raised the challenge of inter-rater reliability, in this case the relative consistency of the judgements (coding) that are made by two or more raters viewing the same segment of video. In many student projects, this may involve what could be called *intra*-rater reliability (i.e. the relative consistency of the judgements – coding – that are made by the same rater viewing the same segment of video multiple times). In either case, the more clearly a code is defined in a coding 'book', database or software package (such as NVivo), the greater the consistency of coding (see Figure 9.1).

Code (node)/ subcode (sub-node)	Definition
Sound	Any noise produced by the child, including vocalising and physical.
Physical sound	Making noises by moving body (e.g. clapping, hitting).
Self-talk	Talking to him/herself.
Vocalising	Any sound produced using mouth (e.g. humming, growling, chanting).

This process highlights a potential drawback to using video data in that the analysis can take a long period of time, with much of the time apparently not seeing much happening, such as a child walking around the woodland without seeing or interacting with anybody. However, a note of caution is needed as this in itself can be data! Another problem with using video with young children is that it is also very difficult to do member checking, sometimes also called respondent or participant validation. Whatever it is called, the aim is to discuss the data you have with participants are 'used to validate, verify, or assess the trustworthi-ness of qualitative results' (Birt et al., 2016: 1802). This is very difficult with young children as they may not have the language, experience or even memory of the event to validate your interpretations. But ethi-cally, every effort should be made to ask them their thoughts if possible.

Figure 9.1 Extract from code book definitions and NVivo screenshot

Finally, although many videos have good sound quality, in the case of children climbing or running it was not always possible to use the data as the sound quality became distorted or muffled, particularly with the body cameras.

INDIVIDUAL/GROUP TASK

Reflect on your own or discuss with others how important member checking is in research with very young children and how you might go about doing this and recording their responses. If you decide to do it or not do it, *why* did you make this decision? This might be, for instance, in relation to the research process, ethics or power relationships.

Dissemination of findings

Having gathered all your data and analysed them, the next step is to use the video, and stills from the video, in dissemination events, such as presenting at a conference, a publication or dissertation. Again, all these possible options need to be considered early in the project so that relevant consent can be gained from all parties.

The advantage of video in our project was that it offered, particularly with the glasses cameras, a unique child's view of the events – you see and hear what they saw and heard. For many audiences, this can be much more interesting than everything else you are saying, however interesting your analysis! Inevitably, though, this will be a small selection of the many hours of video you may have. In contrast, the use of video requires careful consideration of anonymity as the quality of image and sound can lead to concerns about children being identified. These can be alleviated to some extent by being careful throughout the dissemination process – whether in using still photos from the video in a dissertation or playing video in a presentation – to avoid presenting any information that will help with identification. This is a particular challenge as even saying the project used a nursery class in a local school is problematic if the audience (both readers and listeners) know where you are from and there is only one school nearby with a nursery, and only one class in it!

Summary

In this chapter, we have considered the unique contributions that video can make to research in early childhood, particularly outside of the classroom or setting. These include providing a multimodal record of the child's view of the world and their interactions with it. Video can be viewed and listened to repeatedly to allow a more nuanced analysis, both by an individual or research team. Like any digital resource, it can be saved, shared and edited to produce still images or shorter videos for a range of dissemination activities. Conversely, video also presents technical, organisational and ethical challenges, which need to be considered in detail at the start of a research project and revisited throughout, particularly the issue of informed consent and the use of video in disseminating your findings.

Finally, video is only one tool for the researcher and should be used with care to exploit the unique insights it provides, both on its own and in combination with other research tools at our disposal.

Strengths of video as a research tool in early childhood

- Video provides a temporal and sequential record of real events as they unfold.

- Video recording is a natural research method in that it does not require research training.

- Children wearing cameras provide a unique perspective of what they see and hear that cannot be gained any other way.

Limitations of video as a research tool in early childhood

- Member checking is difficult.

- Wearing cameras can be intrusive to children's free play – camera as distractor.

- Ethical challenges throughout the whole research process, from gaining consent to presenting findings.

Recommended reading

Beauchamp, G. and Haughton, C. (2012) Ethics in studying early years. In I. Palaiologou (ed.), *Ethical Practice in Early Childhood*. London: Sage, pp. 147–158.

Cowan, K. (2014) Multimodal transcription of video: examining interaction in early years classrooms. *Classroom Discourse*, 5(1): 6–21.

Schuck, S. and Kearney, M. (2006) Using digital video as a research tool: ethical issues for researchers. *Journal of Educational Multimedia and Hypermedia*, 15(4): 447–463.

References

Adams, D. and Beauchamp, G. (2018) Portals between worlds: a study of the experiences of children aged 7–11 years from primary schools in Wales making music outdoors. *Research Studies in Music Education*, OnlineFirst, http://journals.sagepub.com/doi/pdf/10.1177/1321103X17751251.

Beauchamp, G. and Haughton, C. (2012) Ethics in studying early years. In I. Palaiologou (ed.), *Ethical Practice in Early Childhood*. London: Sage, pp. 147–158.

Birt, L., Scott, S., Cavers, D., Campbell, C. and Walter, F. (2016) Member checking: a tool to enhance trustworthiness or merely a nod to validation? *Qualitative Health Research*, 26(13): 1802–1811.

Coady, M.M. (2001) Ethics in early childhood research. In G. MacNaughton, S.A. Rolfe and I. Siraj-Blatchford (eds), *Doing Early Childhood Research: International Perspectives on Theory and Practice*. Maidenhead: Open University Press, pp. 64–72.

Cowan, K. (2014) Multimodal transcription of video: examining interaction in early years classrooms. *Classroom Discourse*, 5(1): 6–21.

Davies, R. and Hamilton, P. (2018) Assessing learning in the early years' outdoor classroom: examining challenges in practice. *Education 3–13*, 46(1): 117–129.

Deakin, H. and Wakefield, K. (2014) Skype interviewing: reflections of two PhD researchers. *Qualitative Research*, 14(5): 603–616.

Delamont, S. (2002) *Fieldwork in Educational Settings: Methods, Pitfalls and Perspectives*, 2nd edn. London: Routledge.

Derry, S.J., Pea, R.D., Barron, B., Engle, R.A., Erickson, F., Goldman, R., Hall, R., Koschmann, T., Lemke, J.L., Gamoran Sherin, M. and Sherin, B.L. (2010) Conducting video research in the learning sciences: guidance on selection, analysis, technology, and ethics. *The Journal of the Learning Sciences*, 19(1): 3–53.

Dillon, J., Rickinson, M., Teamey, K., Morris, M., Choi, M.Y., Sanders, D. and Benefield, P. (2006) The value of outdoor learning: evidence from research in the UK and elsewhere. *School Science Review*, 87(320): 107–111.

Gylfe, P., Franck, H., Lebaron, C. and Mantere, S. (2016) Video methods in strategy research: focusing on embodied cognition. *Strategic Management Journal*, 37(1): 133–148.

Fisher, J. and Wood, E. (2012) Changing educational practice in the early years through practitioner-led action research: an adult–child interaction project. *International Journal of Early Years Education*, 20(2): 114–129.

Hawxwell, L., O'Shaughnessy, M., Russell, C. and Shortt, D. (2018) 'Do you need a kayak to learn outside?' A literature review into learning outside the classroom. *Education 3–13*, 47(3): 1–11.

Jones, R., Fonseca, J., De Martin Silva, L., Davies, G., Morgan, K. and Mesquita, I. (2016) The promise and problems of video diaries: building on current research. *Qualitative Research in Sport, Exercise and Health*, 7(3): 1–16.

Lacković, N. (2018) Analysing videos in educational research: an 'inquiry graphics' approach for multimodal, Peircean semiotic coding of video data. *Video Journal of Education and Pedagogy*, 3(1): 1–23.

Leung, C. and Hawkins, M. (2011) Video recording and the research process. *TESOL Quarterly*, 45(2): 344–354.

Punch, K.F. and Oancea, A. (2014) *Introduction to Research Methods in Education*, 2nd edn. London: Sage.

Rickinson, M., Dillon, J., Teamey, K., Morris, M., Choi, M.Y., Sanders, D. and Benefield, P. (2004) *A Review of Research on Outdoor Learning*. Preston Montford: Field Studies Council.

Rowan, D., Järkestig-Berggren, U., Cambridge, I., McAuliffe, D., Fung, A. and Moore, M. (2015) The 6 Continents Project: a method for linking social work classrooms for intercultural exchange through asynchronous video sharing. *International Social Work*, 58(4): 484–494.

Schuck, S. and Kearney, M. (2006) Using digital video as a research tool: ethical issues for researchers. *Journal of Educational Multimedia and Hypermedia*, 15(4): 447–463.

Tripp, T.R. and Rich, P.J. (2012) The influence of video analysis on the process of teacher change. *Teaching and Teacher Education: An International Journal of Research and Studies*, 28(5): 728–739.

Van Es, E.A., Tunney, J., Goldsmith, L.T. and Seago, N. (2014) A framework for the facilitation of teachers' analysis of video. *Journal of Teacher Education*, 65(4): 340–356.

Walker, R. (2012) Naturalistic research. In J. Arthur, M. Waring, R. Coe and L.V. Hedges (eds), *Research Methods and Methodologies in Education*. London: Sage, pp. 76–79.

The use of vignettes in research with young children

Ioanna Palaiologou

Introduction

As has been explored elsewhere in this book, research with young children is seeking ways where the agentic nature of childhood is embraced. Researchers are exploring creative and innovative methods to enact participatory research, paying close attention on how to promote the voice of children in research (e.g. Cahill, 2004; Clark and Moss, 2001; Waller and Bitou, 2011). This chapter, based on previous work that drew on different research projects that employed vignettes (hypothetical scenarios that unfold through a series of stages), and by reflecting upon and critically examining to what extent this method is participatory, explores the use of vignettes with young children under the age of 5 to evaluate the use of vignettes as a research tool that enables participation of children (Palaiologou, 2016, 2017).

Vignettes have been used as a research method since the middle of the last century (Herskovits, 1950), and have been used since to mainly examine attitudes, beliefs and values especially around sensitive topics. Their use has been growing in disciplines such as social psychology (Alden et al., 2015), nursing (Hughes and Huby, 2002), social work (O'Dell et al., 2012; Wilks, 2004) and more recently education (Ammann, 2018). Some researchers have started exploring their use with children and young people (Barter and Renold, 2000), but this method has not yet been fully explored as a method in participatory research with young children under the age of 5. Yet vignettes as a research method can offer dialogicality (voice/s) in research with young children (Palaiologou,

2017). Thus, in this chapter, vignettes are explained, as well as their relevance in early childhood research, as a method that has potential to add to the repertoire of participatory methods.

INDIVIDUAL/GROUP TASK

Before you read this chapter, consider what research methods in early childhood that claim participatory nature you are familiar with. What do you think are the advantages and disadvantages of them?

What are vignettes?

Vignettes are defined as 'short stories in written or pictorial form, intended to elicit responses to typical scenarios' (Hill, 1997: 1777), and are used as simulations of real events. These stories based on 'hypothetical characters in specified circumstances' (Finch, 1987: 105) provide 'concrete examples of people and their behaviours on which [participants] can offer comment or opinion. The researcher can then facilitate a discussion around the opinions expressed, or particular terms used in the participants comments' (Hazel, 1995: 2).

All these definitions are summarised on what Bloor and Wood (2006) outline:

> A technique used in structured and in-depth interviews as well as focus groups, providing sketches of fictional (or fictionalized) scenarios. The respondent is then invited to imagine, drawing on his or her own experience, how the central character in the scenario will behave. Vignettes thus collect situated data on group values, group beliefs and group norms of behaviour. While in structured interviews respondents must choose from a multiple-choice menu of possible answers to a vignette, as used in-depth interviews and focus groups, vignettes act as a stimulus to extended discussion of the scenario in question.
>
> (p. 183)

Although vignettes are short scenarios/stories, their form and structure varies, and they are dependent upon the research topic (Hughes and Huby, 2002) and how it relates to the participants (Palaiologou, 2017). Kandemir and Budd (2018) caution us not to be fixated with a static definition of vignettes, but instead to focus on how vignettes are consisted. Vignettes can be a short narrative written story or based on a visual story such as a photograph or an animation. The main principle of a vignette is that participants are not asked to talk about their direct personal experiences, but using the story (visual or written) as a prompt, the participants are asked to talk about a third party. The research participants are offered these scenarios (which can be written on paper or via use of digital technology such as a short film) and are:

> encourage[d] to engage in various acts of orientation and how, through such acts, the researcher is able to gain insight into participants' interpretative processes and the multi-faceted nature of their 'stock of knowledge' (Schutz, 1970) [. . . and participants] can relate them to their own life stories.
>
> (Jenkins et al., 2010: 176)

Among those who examine the use of vignettes in research, there is an agreement that the main purpose of vignettes is to stipulate 'entry points to what can be complex research questions' (Kandemir and Budd, 2018), complex and sensitive situations or topics that participants might otherwise find difficult to discuss and respond to, as in the work of Barter and Renold (2000), who used vignettes with children and young people to investigate violence in residential homes.

Example of vignettes: the views of children with medical conditions on their hospital school

In a recent service evaluation (Mintz et al., 2017) that examined the effectiveness of home and hospital education, one key element in the evaluation was to understand the views of children and young people with medical conditions (physical or mental health) about the service. This evaluation entailed a number of sensitivities and ethical challenges when collecting experiences in their hospital schools from children and young people with medical conditions. After consideration regarding which method can be appropriate, it was decided that it was better that children were not asked to discuss their direct experiences, but asked to discuss the experience in the third person and relate it with their experiences, and hence vignettes were employed. The researchers developed four scenarios based on stories and photographs that were negotiated with the staff from the Hospital and Home Education Services. Due to ethical restrictions, the socio-demographics, as well as the results from the children's data, cannot be reported to a wider audience. The ages of children that took part in the study were from 4 years up to 16. The following examples are two of the vignettes that were developed for children up to the age of 6.

Vignette 1: Aislynn missing school due to illness

The first scenario aimed to capture the views of children that were hospitalised for long periods of time and were pupils of the hospital school. The vignette used a photograph of a young girl (a fictional character, Aislynn, who is 9 years old) in a hospital bed. Next to her is a teacher who wears a medical mask and does some maths activities with the girl. The scenario that was developed was as following:

> Aislynn, 9 years of age, has missed nearly two full years of school while being treated for a chronic intestinal condition.

Then children were shown the photograph and read (if they could) or were told the scenario, with the researcher subsequently asking them to discuss the photo and Aislynn's feelings using the following discussion prompts:

- How do you think Aislynn feels missing her school?

- What do you think is the best way to help Aislynn with her education when she is in hospital?

- What types of lessons do you think Aislynn should have?

- What do you think are the best ways for Aislynn to have lessons when she is in hospital?

- Do you think Aislynn should have lessons when in hospital?

- Do you think Aislynn will like to have lessons in hospital?

- What do you think Aislynn is missing most when in hospital?

- How do you think teachers at the hospital can help Aislynn?

In this way, the children who participated in the project could discuss how it is to deal with a medical condition by attending school in the third person (Aislynn) and not talk about their own personal experiences as this might have placed them in a difficult emotional situation.

Vignette 2: how can we help the Elaine?

In this scenario, where the researchers were interested in the views of children on the role of teachers in a hospital school, the story that was developed was from a teacher. The teacher (fictional character, Elaine) was describing her day in the hospital school and the challenges she might face daily. She also described how the lesson develops while a child is on a hospital bed. She concluded by describing how difficult it is for ill children to attend lessons as they miss their own school and their friends. After the children either read this story or had it told to them, they were asked to discuss the following prompts:

- What do you think is the role of Elaine in the hospital school?

- What lessons do you think Elaine should teach?

- How can Elaine make the lesson enjoyable?

- How can Elaine make the child's day interesting?

- How can Elaine help the child with the lessons?

- How can Elaine help the child to be in touch with the school they attended prior to hospitalisation?

- What do you think would have made the lesson more interesting and enjoyable?

- What do you think could be done so the children can keep connected with their friends?

- What do you think could be done so the children can keep connected with their school and classroom?

Using this story, children were able to discuss what effective teaching is in the hospital school from their point of view by discussing Elaine and not their own personal experiences (but based on them) or their own teachers.

Vignettes, as in the examples above, help researchers to stimulate discussion on the research topic by:

> creating a distance between the context of the vignette and the participant, by not asking people directly about their own experiences, rather by asking how third parties might feel, act, or to be advised to proceed in a given situation.
>
> (Kandemir and Budd, 2018)

However, to ensure the validity of the research, the vignettes need to be directly linked with the research topic and with the objectives of the topic under investigation, as well as to be directly relevant to the experiences of the participants that the researcher tries to elicit. Finally, they must be developed into a language (written or visual) that is appropriate to the participants, so participants can conceive the context in which the story takes place, so, based on their experiences and their views, they can respond to how the characters in the story might react, rather than discuss directly their own experiences (Hughes and Huby, 2004; Jenkins et al., 2010).

In early childhood research, and especially with growing emphasis on participatory ideology in research with children, the use of this method can offer an alternative, and 'can help strike balance and address some of the ethical and methodological issues of research with children' (Punch, 2002: 337). Also, it can offer an alternative method to investigate with young children research topics that are sensitive, such as illness and violence, or abstract issues, such as well-being and resilience.

INDIVIDUAL/GROUP TASK

Can you think of any topics in research with young children that will be challenging to research due to their sensitivities or ethical challenges? What are the advantages of not asking directly about children's experiences?

The use of vignettes

As discussed above, researchers have explored the forms that these vignettes can take. For example, they can either be written stories shared in paper or via a tablet, or pictorial such as photographs, short films of a real-life situation or animations. They can be in the form of a 'snapshot' (Bloor, 1991) or a story that is developed and unfolds in stages, where 'participants are typically asked to respond to these stories with what they would do in particular situation on how they think a third person would respond' (Hughes, 1998: 381) at the various stages as the story progresses.

For example, Jenkins et al. (2010) made use of interactive vignettes. They constructed:

> a series of scenarios on Microsoft PowerPoint slides then hyper-linking potential courses of action on those slides to the slides relevant to those actions. In this way, it was possible for participants to influence how the scenario would unfold, as they would only see the slides that were relevant to the courses of action they selected. Furthermore, as routes through the scenario were not fixed it was possible to chart participants' courses of action and then compare them with those of other interviewees.
>
> (p. 189)

As was mentioned earlier, vignette form is not static, and researchers cannot be engrossed by the format of the vignettes, but should instead focus on their content. Instead, high importance should be placed on the relevance of the vignettes to the research topic and its participants. Having this in mind, when applying vignettes with young children they can be altered from the traditional formats that the literature cited here has examined with older children and young people (for more, see Palaiologou, 2017). In the example below, the use of a different vignette is explored with young children.

Vignette 3: my journey from home to nursery

This example is based on a research project with 3- to 5-year-old children that used vignettes (Palaiologou, 2016). The focus of the research was to investigate how children at this age understand the notion of the community around them and how they see themselves in their community. There were four nurseries involved in this project. Two of them were in close proximity to the city centre of the area that the project took place, and the other two in the suburbs of the city. There were 25 children taking part in the project. The research project was explained to children in a way that was age-appropriate, child-friendly and not abstract. They were given the following story:

> John is 3.5 years old. When he leaves his home every day to go to the nursery, he walks with his mother, but John feels very sad as he does not see anything or anyone else on his way to nursery apart from houses.

The prompt question was:

> How do you think John can make his journey more interesting?

With this vignette as a prompt, the aim was to elicit children's experiences from their own journeys to school in an attempt to see to what extent children understand that there is a community around them and who they think are part of this community (e.g. the post office, the local convenience store, the lollipop person, the other parents who walk with their children).

The children in the project were quick to start drawing upon their own journeys to nursery, and in one group they decided to make cards to send to John telling him their own journeys. They decided that John could get one card every day and read it. This way, he might 'share' his journey with another child and would not feel so bored. These are some of the examples that children drew to send to John.

In Figure 10.1, Emily (4 years) described to the researcher that she leaves home every day and stops at the local store where her mother buys her a bread roll. Then she goes straight to school, but she said that sometimes her mother also stops at the petrol station behind the local store.

In Figure 10.2, Nathan (4 years and 6 months), when he was doing his card, described the journey to the researcher not how it really was, but how he wanted it to be, and although the real journey is in the car from home to nursery, he imagined a number of stops (such as the swimming pool, the park, his friend's house and his cousin's house). He asked that we call his card 'My Neighbourhood' instead of 'My Journey to Nursery'.

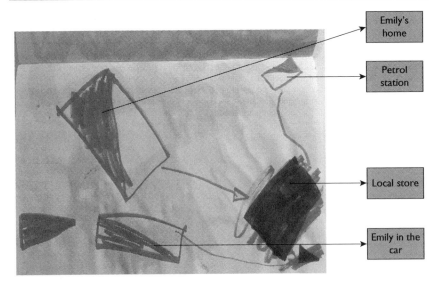

Figure 10.1 Emily's journey from home to nursery

In this project, it was found that children at this age have a sense of the existence of neighbourhood (immediate community), but the sense of being part of it is still being developed. In this project, the vignette method helped the researchers to discuss an abstract topic with a relevant example for the children, and in a language that was understood by them.

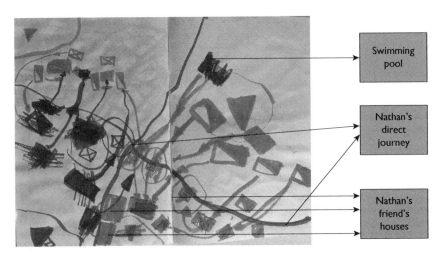

Figure 10.2 Nathan's neighbourhood

The use of vignettes in this project engaged children not only to participate, but also engage, explore and identify a topic (such as their sense of community, which is abstract) that may have remained untapped using other standard methods such as interviews or observations.

INDIVIDUAL/GROUP TASK

Before reading the next section, what do you think are the strengths of using vignettes with young children? Can you think of any limitations?

Why vignettes?

As mentioned above, vignettes offer us entry points to research questions that are complex, abstract and deal with sensitive situations. One of the key advantages to using this method with young children, where the stories are offered in a language that is understood from the children, is that it can elicit personal meaning(s), as was shown in the examples of Emily and Nathan. Also, as the context of these scenarios is familiar to the context of the children, they can feel at ease to start talking about a third person rather than about themselves, especially to researchers that children are not always familiar with.

However, I have found from using this approach that children tend to move from the character to self, and start talking about their personal experiences by merging multiple emotions (such as affection, fondness and anger) and real-life experiences with aspirational experiences (as in the case of Nathan's real journey and the journey he wanted to do) in their responses to the vignettes.

As was shown in the examples above, the vignettes, when they are designed in a language relevant to the children, become simpler and manageable for them, and by focusing on individual data (each child's lived experience) can offer insights into children's lives, and subsequently facilitate the exploration of the individual's voice. As vignettes focus on each child's lived experiences, the data are authentic and locally relevant, thus allowing the researcher to reflect children's own voices in relation to their experiences rather than to the adults.

Finally, it is important to emphasise here that vignettes have limitations as children might offer socially accepted responses to the scenarios; there are no homogenous data, and the researcher ends up with a variety of data that entails challenges for validity, reliability and generalisations. Also, as they rely on responses on values, beliefs and experiences, it needs to be noted that the responses from the vignettes entail emotional subjectivity.

To conclude, although the aim is to create a distance between the context of the story presented in the vignette and the children (so they will not feel threatened to discuss directly their own personal experiences to unfamiliar people), it was found that children speedily personalise the stories and start discussing their own experiences (Palaiologou, 2016, 2017). This can be a limitation in terms of the subjectivity of the data. However, in qualitive research with young children that is concerned directly with people's personal narratives and understanding of beliefs, values and experiences, it can offer a real strength. For all those reasons, it is suggested here that it is advisable in research with young children that vignettes should be used with and/or be incorporated into other research methods. This will offer richer data that can be cross-referenced for validity and reliability purposes.

INDIVIDUAL/GROUP TASK

Jenkins et al. (2010) frame vignettes as acts of perceptual orientation in which participants may offer their thoughts and their positions to describe and analyse their data. Reflecting on this view, what methodological challenges might need to be acknowledged using vignettes?

Conclusions

As discussed elsewhere in the book (see Chapters 4 and 5, this volume), researching young children within participatory lenses has challenges. Early childhood research is interested in the lived experiences of the children and in developing a dialogical process in the research. So, it is concluded that the use of vignettes in participatory research offers methodological and ethical advantages to the researchers.

Vignettes offer opportunities to explore children's beliefs, responses, actions in certain researched contexts, and social situations in participants' own terms, thus putting children in control of to what extent they choose to disclose personal information or carry on discussing issues from a 'non-personal less threatening perspective' (Hughes, 1998: 383). As was discussed throughout this chapter, vignettes allow participants to discuss, explore, express situations and social phenomena in their own terms, and moreover encourage dialogicality. At the methodological level, reflecting on the above, vignettes empower children to be always in control (on their own terms) to the level of their engagement, as well as to the extent they will reveal personal information. The quest for participatory research thus requires a methodology where children are empowered to be in control of the research process, the voice(s) of children to be included at all stages of the research, and 'subjective experiences to emerge' (Palaiologou, 2017: 319). Thus, it is suggested that vignettes, although little attention has been paid as a research method in early childhood research, should be seen as a participatory method. At an ethical level, the main strength of vignettes is that sensitive or complex topics can be discussed in less personal and less threatening ways for young children.

To conclude, it has not been the intention to say that participatory ideology cannot be achieved with the use of other research methods, but to demonstrate that the use of vignettes in research with young children can be a valuable method among the available methods to researchers. However, its use in early childhood research has not yet been explored fully. It has been shown that the key characteristics of vignettes are in line with participatory ideology at the methodological and ethical levels, and as such they can become an alternative and innovative research method as they elicit data from children's lived experiences in their own terms.

Summary

■ Vignettes are 'stories about individuals, situations and structures which can make reference to important points in the study of perceptions, beliefs and attitudes [. . .] Participants are typically asked to respond to these stories with what they would do in a particular situation or how they think a third person would respond' (Hughes, 1998: 381).

- The use of vignettes with children under 5 has still not been explored as part of the participatory ideology in research.

- Vignettes aim to introduce topics in research that responders might otherwise find difficult to discuss (Herskovits, 1950).

- Vignettes allow *actions in context* to be explored, to clarify people's judgements and to provide a less personal, and therefore less threatening, way of exploring sensitive topics (Barter and Renold, 1999).

- Vignettes allow participants to discuss, explore and express situations and social phenomena *in their own terms*.

- Vignette methodology allows researchers to systematically explore issues that could potentially be sensitive to research participants, as it allows participants to control whether they disclose personal information or not, and to discuss issues from a 'non-personal and therefore less threatening perspective' (Hughes, 1998: 383).

Recommended reading

Although the papers suggested below are not directly linked with early childhood research, they will help you understand how vignettes are used in research:

Hughes, R. and Huby, M. (2004) The construction and interpretation of vignettes in social research. *Social Work & Social Sciences Review*, 11(1): 36–51.

Jenkins, N., Bloor, M., Fischer, J., Berney, L. and Neale, J. (2010) Putting it into context: the use of vignettes in qualitative interviewing. *Qualitative Research*, 10(2): 175–198.

This paper is based on a methodological discussion of vignettes in early childhood research:

Palaiologou, I. (2017) The use of vignettes in participatory research with young children. *International Journal of Early Years Education*, 25(3): 308–322.

References

Alden, D.L., Friend, J.M., Lee, A.Y., de Vries, M., Osawa, R. and Chen, Q. (2015) Culture and medical decision making: healthcare consumer perspectives in Japan and the United States. *Health Psychology*, 34(12), 1133–1144.

Ammann, M. (2018) Leadership for learning as experience: introducing the use of vignettes for research on leadership experience in schools. *International Journal of Qualitative Methods*, 17: 1–13.

Barter, C. and Renold, E. (1999) The use of vignettes in qualitative research. *Social Research Update*, 25: 1–7.

Barter, C. and Renold, E. (2000) 'I wanna tell you a story': exploring the application of vignettes in qualitative research with children and young people. *International Journal of Social Research Methodology*, 3(4): 307–323.

Bloor, M. (1991) A minor office: the variable and socially constructed character of death certification in a Scottish city. *Journal of Health & Social Behaviour*, 32(3): 273–287.

Bloor, M. and Wood, F. (2006) *Keywords in Qualitative Methods: A Vocabulary of Research Concepts*. London: Sage.

Cahill, C. (2004) Defying gravity? Raising consciousness through collective research. *Children's Geographies*, 2(2): 273–286.

Clark, A. and Moss, P. (2001) *Listening to Young Children: The Mosaic Approach*. London: National Children's Bureau.

Finch, J. (1987) The vignette technique in survey research. *Sociology*, 21(1): 105–114.

Hazel, N. (1995) Elicitation techniques with young people. *Social Research Update*, 12, Department of Sociology, University of Surrey. Available at: http://sru.soc.surrey.ac.uk/SRU12.html (accessed 15 March 2019).

Herskovits, M.J. (1950) The hypothetical situation: a technique of field research. *Journal of Anthropology*, 6: 32–40.

Hill, M. (1997) Research review: participatory research with children. *Child and Family Social Work*, 2: 171–183.

Hughes, R. (1998) Considering the vignette technique and its application to a study of drug injecting and HIV risk and safer behaviour. *Sociology of Health and Illness*, 20: 381–400.

Hughes, R. and Huby, M. (2002) The application of vignettes in social and nursing research. *Journal of Advanced Nursing*, 37(4), 382–386.

Hughes, R. and Huby, M. (2004) The construction and interpretation of vignettes in social research. *Social Work & Social Sciences Review*, 11(1): 36–51.

Jenkins, N., Bloor, M., Fischer, J., Berney, L. and Neale, J. (2010) Putting it into context: the use of vignettes in qualitative interviewing. *Qualitative Research*, 10(2): 175–198.

Kandemir, A. and Budd, R. (2018) Using vignettes to explore reality and values with young people *Forum Qualitative Sozialforschung/Forum: Qualitative Social Research*, 19(2): Art. 1, http://dx.doi.org/10.17169/fqs-19.2.2914.

Mintz, J., Palaiologou, I. and Caroll, C. (2017) *An Independent Review to Inform Best Practice for the Future Educational Provision for Children Unable to Attend School for Medical Reasons*. London: University College London, Institute of Education.

O'Dell, L., Crafter, S., de Abreu, G. and Cline, T. (2012) The problem of interpretation in vignette methodology in research with young people. *Qualitative Research*, 12(6): 702–714.

Palaiologou, I. (2016) *The Use of Vignettes in Research with Young Children*. Paper presented at the 26th Annual European Early Childhood Education Research Association Conference, 31 August–3 September 2016, Dublin, Ireland.

Palaiologou, I. (2017) The use of vignettes in participatory research with young children. *International Journal of Early Years Education*, 25(3): 308–322.

Punch, S. (2002) Research with children: the same or different from research with adults? *Childhood*, 9(3): 321–341.

Schutz, A. (1970) *Reflections on the Problem of Relevance*. New Haven, CT: Yale University Press.

Waller, T. and Bitou, A. (2011) Research with children: three challenges for participatory research in early childhood. *European Early Childhood Education Research Journal*, 19(1): 5–20.

Wilks, T. (2004) The use of vignettes in qualitative research into social work values. *Qualitative Social Work*, 3(1): 78–87.

PART III

Researching with practitioners and parents

The use of identity boxes as a research method

Helen Perkins

Introduction

In this chapter, the effectiveness of using artefacts and creative activities in focus groups is explored. Drawing on my doctoral research with early childhood education and care (ECEC), student-practitioners, examples of how identity boxes were used to facilitate reflexive opportunities to enhance the account of the participants' experiences (Pink, 2007). The chapter then considers how using creative activities and the use of objects provides the opportunity for participants to reflect on the key events or critical incidents and to reconfigure and reorder them into the story they want to tell (Pink, 2007). Clark-Keefe (2009) states, 'Often, I can see it before I can say it. I can sense it before I can make sense of it linguistically' (p. 17); it is the application of this concept that underpins the method. This chapter draws on examples from two research projects: the first, *Creative Research Methods in a College-Based Higher Education Setting* (Kendall and Perkins, 2014); the second, from Helen's own doctoral study, which is entitled *From Training to Qualification: The Journey of Level 3 Early Years Student-Practitioners* (Perkins, 2017), and examines the efficacy of identity boxes as a methodological tool. The chapter concludes with a discussion of the strengths and challenges of using creative activities as a research method.

What are identity boxes?

Identity boxes or story boxes are craft-based creations constructed by participants that act as a provocation for facilitating and supporting the reflexive process, providing a basis for thinking critically about our experiences, values and actions (see Figure 11.1). Stories from the past can often be connected to objects, and the object is then able to evoke memories (Pahl and Rowsell, 2010: 8). This research method enables time for reflexivity, which produces rich data, in contrast to a direct questioning approach (e.g. interviews), which do not allow time for reflection; as Gauntlett (2007) observed, most people do not respond well to a sociologist with a clipboard.

Getting started

When considering any data collection instrument, careful preparation is needed. In the same way you prepare your interview or survey questions in advance, similarly you will need to prepare when using a creative method. You will need to collect resources and plan where the activity will take place. It is difficult to do a pilot study with this method; however, you might want to create your own identity box to run through the process. This will help you to decide if the

Figure 11.1 Example of an identity box

chosen environment works and whether you have the right sort of resources available. There are a variety of materials that can be used (see Figure 11.2). These include:

- shoeboxes or other similar-sized boxes;

- a selection of craft materials, including, scissors, sticky tape and glue sticks;

- camera and audio recording equipment; and

- a project information sheet and ethical consent forms, which include permission to record and to photograph.

The process

Identity boxes are used within the context of a focus group, which is a qualitative research technique used by researchers to gather opinions of a small number of participants who come together to discuss a particular topic or issue. Krueger and Casey (2015) highlight focus groups as an effective method to collect qualitative data where the participants are similar

Figure 11.2 Example of possible materials

in their perspective. There are many aspects to consider when using identity boxes as a method for collecting data. The environment needs to be prepared before participants arrive, ensuring you have sufficient craft resources available. I have used Lego as an alternative to craft materials, and it works equally as well and may be more appealing to some participants. You will need to consider the age, cohesion and experience of your group. Participants may be sharing personal experiences; therefore, it is essential that they feel confident to express their ideas within the group.

INDIVIDUAL/GROUP TASK

Consider your own research question and your participants. Might this be a useful method for your research? How might you use this method in your own research? What might be a barrier to using this approach?

Setting the task

Having completed the consent forms, the task is then set. In both projects when I have used identity boxes, the starting point was for students to reflect on their own journey to becoming a practitioner. This approach positions students as both the researcher and the researched (Kendall and Perkins, 2014). 'The role of the researcher is to inhabit an evidentiary middle space, gathering empirical material while engaging in dialogues that help avoid premature considerations of their understandings and explanations' (Kamberelis and Dimitriadis, 2011: 548). There is the potential for focus groups to produce weak evidence (Kamberelis and Dimitriadis, 2011). I discuss my own experience of this later in this chapter. When setting the task in my own projects, the directions are deliberately loose and open to interpretation by each participant:

> We would, we suggested, make objects; tell stories; listen to stories; discuss our object and storymaking; curate and share symbolic objects; take pictures and audio recordings; and discuss our thoughts and feelings uninhibited by research conventions, interviews, structure or systematisation along the way.
>
> (Kendall and Perkins, 2014: 5)

The research method and data collection instrument sits within an auto-ethnographic (and ethnographic) approach as it elicits the telling of small stories, what Lyotard (1979) calls 'petit récit'.

Rather than a time limit, I suggest reviewing progress after 20 minutes. In both projects where I used identity boxes, the activity took around 40 minutes. Participants are sharing personal stories; therefore, it is important to remind participants that the 'Chatham House Rule' applies – when a meeting is held under the Chatham House Rule, participants are free to use the information received, but neither the identity nor the affiliation of the speaker(s), nor that of any other participant, may be revealed (Chatham House, 2002). This allows for open discussion within the group, with agreement from all participants to maintain confidentiality and ethical practice.

Once the boxes are complete (see Figure 11.3), participants share their stories; with permission, recording the stories assists with accuracy in the analysis process. Once the stories have been transcribed, they should be checked for accuracy and reconfirmation of participants' permission for the data to be used (Cohen et al., 2011). Collecting data in this way appeared to lead to a relaxed atmosphere and participants may have been less inhibited. This may have led to disclosures of personal information that were unintended. Consequently, going through the process of member checking is even more important. Checking that participants are satisfied with their transcripts is an important ethical consideration in all research projects.

Figure 11.3 Examples of assembled boxes from project 2

The value of using creative methods

Every picture tells a story; this is the premise for the use of identity boxes as a qualitative, creative research method. The notion of using a creative provocation to provide a vehicle for reflection appealed to me in my research with mature students studying an Early Years Foundation Degree (Kendall and Perkins, 2014) and again with 16- to 19-year-old Early Years National Diploma students (Perkins, 2017). In each project, the aim was to explore the students' journeys to professional formation using identity boxes to facilitate personal narratives, and as a means of supporting the reflexive process. The notion of visual ethnography is well documented by Pink (2012) in her book *Doing Visual Ethnography*, in Gauntlett (2007) and Gauntlett and Awan (2011), who explored how young people use media in shaping their identities. Similarly, Clark-Keefe (2009) used art as a means of exploring gender and class subjectivity in her own auto-ethnography, and her research participants' experiences. She sees art, in all its forms, as the 'critical companions to linguistic expression' (p. 24).

Identity boxes as a methodological tool

Identity boxes are a versatile research method that complement qualitative and interpretivist paradigms. My aim was to enable students to articulate the knowledge, skills, attitudes and dispositions they have acquired through their experiences. Using identity boxes is participatory, which for me seemed to suggest doing research 'with' rather than 'on' my participants. Experiences and concepts were examined through the eyes of the individual participants. Consequently, personal narratives, experiences and opinions are valuable data, and the methods used to harvest these stories are legitimised as a qualitative research tool (see Chapter 12, this volume).

Denzin and Lincoln (2011) suggest that 'qualitative researchers study things in their natural settings, attempting to make sense of, or to interpret, phenomena in terms of the meaning people bring to them' (p. 3). In the application of this method, a third space position of para-autoethnography was adopted. That is, a space between ethnography, in which we study others, and auto-ethnography, in which we study ourselves (Gauntlett, 2007; Gee, 2000). Using this approach, there is an 'inversion of expertise' where it is the storyteller, not the listener, who is the 'expert in the field' (Ellis, 2004: 14) In the two project examples, the participants told and interpreted their own journeys, which could be considered auto-ethnography; however, as the researcher and author, it was my version of their narratives that was written, firmly situating identity boxes as a research tool in an interpretivist paradigm (Punch, 2006; Wellington, 2000).

In both research projects, in the making of the boxes and in the telling and retelling of their stories, students made meaning of their reflections. In doing so, students gained an understanding of the experiences they have had, and how these experiences have shaped their understanding of their journey into ECEC practice. Kress's (2011) 'REDO cycle' – reveal, examine, dismantle, open – was used to provide a strategy for co-constructing the meanings about the students' journeys of being and becoming ECEC practitioners.

Constructing and revisiting the boxes enabled the students to (re) construct their stories and, as Kress (2011) suggests, challenged my own understanding of their experiences, arguing that 'stepping out' of traditional research methods allows the researcher to engage with others who see the world differently. In the following section, examples are shared from the two projects, beginning with ethical considerations.

Ethical considerations

The personal, sensitive and collaborative nature, and therefore public nature, of this research approach meant that there were significant ethical considerations associated with using identity boxes. There is the potential for the reflexive nature of the activity to raise feelings and memories that may be upsetting to recall. And indeed, this did occur when one participant in my study (Perkins, 2017) reflected on a negative school experience that had affected her GCSE grades, and therefore her lack of progression opportunities.

Before commencing, as with the use of any research tool, a discussion with your participants to explain the process and how their data will be used is essential. Whether they are to be used in your dissertation or for any research, it is vital that you make clear to your participants how their data will be used, kept safe and disseminated. As you will have read in other chapters, obtaining ethical approval from your institution is essential; this will help you identify any ethical issues and require you to consider how you may ameliorate them. Gaining informed consent is essential, and consideration must be given to confidentiality and anonymity. Participants are sharing personal and confidential stories that may be identifiable. It is important to agree to the use of appropriate pseudonyms for the participants and for people and places they may mention. When using photographs, you will need to ensure you have permission to include identifiable features or agree that you will blur them out in any published material. Participants must be informed of their right to withdraw from the research. A more detailed discussion of informed consent and ethical considerations when designing your research project can be found in Chapter 2, this volume.

There are some specific ethical considerations for using identity boxes. For example, in the first project, I explored Foundation Degree students' perceptions of their learning journey in higher education. At the time of the research, I was their head of school; my position meant that I was accountable/responsible for the students' experience on their course. This had the potential to inhibit the students' responses, thus reducing the quality of the data. The inevitable power relationship between researcher and participants needs to be carefully considered to reduce the possibility of ethical tensions developing (Nutbrown, 2018). It is important to agree ground rules if participants are to feel confident to be open and honest, without feeling that there may be consequences (e.g. if they gave negative feedback on their experiences in college). Students may have felt obligated to participate. They could have been concerned about whether their contributions would affect their grades if their responses were inappropriate or lacking in knowledge and understanding. This was a very real concern for these Foundation Degree students as the research was embedded in their research methods module, and therefore could impact on their grades. In both projects, I inhabited multiple roles, as researcher, lecturer, ECEC practitioner and academic. Sultana (2007) suggests that embodying multiple roles creates tensions for researchers. My research participants are ECEC student-practitioners; therefore, it could be argued, as I am a qualified ECEC practitioner, that I approach my research as an 'insider' conversely, as a manager, lecturer and academic, that I am viewed as an outsider (Merriam et al., 2001). Researcher positionality should be considered in each of the roles in relation to your participants (positionality is discussed in detail in Chapter 1, this volume).

INDIVIDUAL/GROUP TASK

Reflect on Sultana's (2007) assertion that embodying multiple roles can create tension. What roles will you embody in your research? How might they create tension between you and your participants?

Identity boxes in research

Project 1: creative research methods in a college-based higher education setting

This research began with a serendipitous meeting with Alex Kendall from Birmingham City University to discuss possible opportunities to work together on a Higher Education Academy funded research project exploring the teaching of research methods in higher education. I had just read Cathy Nutbrown's (2011) paper 'A Box of Childhood', in which she used carefully selected artefacts from her childhood to facilitate reflection as she wondered about how she found her way into a career in early childhood education. At the same time, I was teaching a research methods module to Early Years Foundation Degree students, and, inspired by Nutbrown's paper, I wanted the students to think differently, to look beyond the conventional methods of interviews and questionnaires. We attempted to 'push out from the safe(er) boundaries of established methodologies' (Nutbrown, 2011: 241) and challenged ourselves to developing innovative methods for teaching research methods in higher education.

The research had a dual purpose: learning about research to support the students' module learning, and to prepare them for their level 6 project. Identity boxes were used as a research method as well as a teaching method to support their learning about the research process. The dual purpose of the project allowed for students to learn about research by doing research, rather than research as an abstract concept; 'as such, learning is embodied and experiential' (Kendall and Perkins, 2014).

The use of identity boxes facilitated deep reflection and generated primary data for the student-researchers. They became the data, for which we then co-constructed meanings around identity, purpose and processes. The stories were rich and offered an insight into the many and varied routes into the early childhood sector, and subsequently to the Foundation Degree. There were many metaphors in the boxes (e.g. brick walls), which represented barriers that students had overcome (e.g. Donna used scales to show the struggle balancing family, work and study) (see Figure 11.4).

Students acknowledged the importance of family support and encouragement. One of the students talked about being a role model for her grandchildren, while expressing her amazement at being on the Foundation Degree at all, adding that she very definitely would not continue to the BA honours top-up year. She had, she felt, reached her limit academically and personally, and wanted to reclaim her place in the family.

Figure 11.4 Donna: balancing family, work and study

Before the second session, students were asked to read 'A Box of Childhood' (Nutbrown, 2011) and to bring an artefact that represented their route to the Foundation Degree. There were again some fascinating stories; however, for me, there seemed a more guarded discussion, something more curated and managed, rather than the spontaneity of the previous week. I perceived a competitive edge; perhaps some students felt pressure to have a 'really interesting' story to present, perhaps thinking about the stories Alex and I might want to hear? It put me in mind of Margaret Donaldson's (1978) criticism of Piaget's conservation tasks, in which she argued that the repetition of the task was interpreted by the children as giving the wrong answer the first time. Did we affect the outcome by repeating the activity, albeit in a different format? In the future, I would only use one creative data collection instrument in a project. That said, the impact of the initial activity produced rich data that contributed to the literature on the early childhood workforce and the value of higher education.

One of the aims of this project was to develop the students' knowledge about research. Their learning is something that should be kept in mind, whatever research method you use, but it is particularly pertinent to any method that investigates the deeply personal.

Whether this response is replicable is impossible to say. This was a cohesive group who had been together for two years. I would suggest that this is an essential factor for this type of activity; there is a need for trust between the group and the researcher to create an environment in which participants feel safe and their confidentiality respected.

For this project, there were additional outcomes beyond learning about the participants' journey:

- Students learned to see participants as people, not data.

- They were mindful to be respectful when intimate and personal stories were being shared.

- They found listening to others 'humbling' and felt honoured to have been privy to those very private stories.

- Having asked their question, they respectfully listened and responded to the answers.

■ They felt the responsibility of responding to difficult and emotive content.

■ When reflecting on identity boxes as a research tool, the students agreed that the boxes and artefacts enriched their stories and helped in developing the narrative.

Project 2: from training to qualification – the journey of level 3 early years student-practitioners

In this, my doctoral research, I aimed to develop a coherent understanding of how the full-time level 3 students' concept of the role of the ECEC practitioner changed from the beginning of their course to their entry in to employment; aiming to identify the benefits of being qualified. I used identity boxes as a research tool in conjunction with an online survey and interviews. The survey had produced key data regarding the respondents' understanding of the role of the ECEC practitioner, but had not addressed how undertaking their qualification had shaped that understanding. This was to be the focus of the identity box activity.

Participants who were about to complete their course were invited to join the focus group (seven students took part). Students were asked to reflect on the time they had spent in college and consider how their qualification had shaped their understanding of being an ECEC practitioner. I was initially 'disappointed' as the stories generated lacked the richness and reflexivity of the Foundation Degree students' responses; the stories were shorter and less reflective.

AN INITIALLY SHORT STORY: FRANCESCA'S STORY

I started when I came to college – I came here basically similar to Bob, mine started when my little brother was born I knew that I wanted to work with children since I have come here I've done my Level 2 and 3 and got a job and I've gained loads knowledge that I didn't have when I first started.

I considered if this was a failing on my part by not probing more deeply, or is it the case that reflectivity (which is discussed in detail in Chapter 2, this volume) is a skill that requires maturity? Reflecting on my earlier comment about the cohesion and maturity of the Foundation Degree group, perhaps the age and experience of this younger group was a factor; this may be due to the psychological and social change in teenagers' brains. Christie and Viner (2005) suggest that teenagers can feel self-conscious, particularly when engaging in an adult world. I proffer there is a tacit understanding that academic research is a very adult activity.

As mentioned previously, the method is 'unstructured'. Following the creation of the boxes and the telling of the stories, a discussion ensued as the participants were very interested in the similarities and differences in their experience; it was this unstructured discussion, prompted by the activity, that produced rich and useful data. For example, there was an animated conversation regarding the quality of some placements. Their examples of unprofessional behaviours and practices evidenced their own learning journey as practitioners and their understanding of professional practice. The creative process had acted as a catalyst for the more in-depth reflection I had hoped for. Fortunately, this was recorded, and participants agreed for this to be included in the data.

I had assumed that, as the head of school, the person managing the curriculum, I knew about the students and their experiences while on their course. I had known them for three years, more in some instances. I had expectations of the outcome. This process highlighted, when looking though a different lens (Brookfield, 1995), that the students' experiences were very different to my perception. For example, in Lee's story (see Figure 11.5), I had not appreciated the impact on her being 'called into the head's office'. She reflected how angry she felt at being there 'often'. Her journey was full of highs and lows (the white line). As time went by, she came to appreciate how her understanding of being 'in the head's office' changed over time. Rather than a place of discipline, a place to fear, it became a non-judgemental space for her to reflect and to collect her thoughts and prepare to re-enter the learning environment. She represented this using Post-its showing the diminishing size of the office.

For Amelia, studying was a stressful process (see Figure 11.6), yet I would never have known it. She was a model student: excellent attendance and timekeeping, very good in placement, well organised, and her coursework completed to a good standard. Yet listening to her articulate her journey with emotion, expression, intonation and body language, I now know this is the result of her 'blood, sweat and tears' (Perkins, 2017).

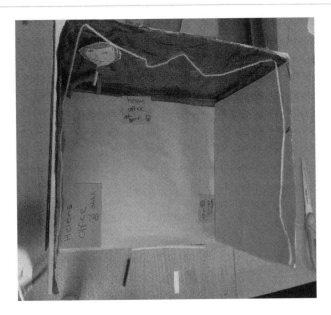

Figure 11.5 Lee's identity box

Figure 11.6 Amelia's identity box

There are many more examples in my thesis; however, there is limited space here to do justice to all of my participants' stories. I am grateful to those who allowed me to share their contributions to the research. There are strengths and limitations to all research methods;

drawing on my reflections on both projects, here are the key points for using identity boxes.

Strengths and limitations of using identify boxes as a research tool

Strengths

- The identity box process acts as a catalyst for deep reflection.

- The nature of collecting data in this way appeared to lead to a relaxed atmosphere and put participants at ease.

- The method produces rich, contextualised data, including participants' feelings and moods.

- The relationship between the researcher and the participants is strengthened.

- The creative approach can be non-threatening.

- The process values participants as individuals, not just data.

Limitations

- The method takes time to plan and prepare resources and negotiate time limits. This can be challenging as once you have set the task to ask participants, to stop can limit the depth of their reflections, impacting on the quality of the data.

- A potential limitation is that the identity box may be interpreted differently by the researcher compared to the participants. It is essential that the participants have the time and opportunity to explain their creations.

- When setting the task, the examples discussed earlier have shown that participants make their own sense of the task. Be prepared to be flexible.

- Participating in creative methods, including identity boxes, requires participants to want to and to be able to physically engage with this approach.

■ Participants and researchers must be mindful to be respectful when intimate and personal stories are being shared. It is important, having asked your question, to respectfully listen and respond to the answers. There is a responsibility to respond appropriately to difficult and emotive content.

■ The stories told may include others not involved in the research; there will be ethical considerations to be considered in how they are included or excluded.

■ This is not a method for everyone; it is important to know your group as there can be unintended and unexpected outcomes. This is not a method for highly sensitive or emotive subjects.

Conclusion

Using creative methods requires time and space, as well as participants willing to engage in a creative process. As with all research methods, the data collected represent what your participants want you to know. In both projects, as participants began the activity, they gathered a selection of resources and chatted as they enjoyed the creativity of the task. After about 8 to 10 minutes, they returned items to the craft trolley and began looking carefully for specific items. I was reminded of Nutbrown's (2011) process of selecting and rejecting the objects for her 'A Box of Childhood', prioritising the stories she wished to tell. The room became quiet as participants became absorbed in the task of creating their boxes. What makes identity boxes an effective research instrument is the space and time for participants to think, reflect and (re)construct their stories. While the stories are not necessarily 'truthful', it is a representation of how your participants' understanding of a concept or experience is, at that moment in time. In conclusion, I argue that identity boxes were an effective means of facilitating a greater understanding of the students' conceptualisations of their journey, their identity and their experiences in early childhood education and care, and as such are valuable in qualitative research.

Summary

In this chapter, I have demonstrated the use of identity boxes as a method for collecting rich, thick data that elicit an insight into participants' understanding of complex ideas or experiences. Identity boxes are an effective way of enhancing a focus group discussion, providing thinking space and time for participants to formulate the story they wish to tell:

- Participants and researchers must be mindful to be respectful when intimate and personal stories are being shared.

- When reflecting on identity boxes as a research tool, the students agreed that the boxes and artefacts enriched their stories and helped in developing the stories.

- It is important, having asked your question, to respectfully listen and respond to the answers.

- There is a responsibility to respond appropriately to difficult and emotive content.

- When setting the task, the examples discussed earlier have shown that participants make their own sense of the task. Be prepared to be flexible.

- It's not a method for everyone – it is important to know your group.

- There can be unintended and unexpected outcomes – this is not a method for highly sensitive or emotive subjects.

Recommended reading

Gauntlett, D. (2007) *Creative Explorations: New Approaches to Identities and Audiences.* London: Routledge.

Gee, P. (2000) Identity as an analytic lens for research in education. *Review of Research in Education*, 25: 99–125.

Kendall, A. and Perkins, H. (2014) *Creative Research Methods in a College-Based Higher Education Setting.* York: Higher Education Academy.

Kendall, A., Gibson, M., Himsworth, C., Palmer, K. and Perkins, H. (2016) Listening to old wives' tales: small stories and the (re)making and (re)telling of research in HE/FE practitioner education. *Research in Post-Compulsory Education*, 21(1–2): 116–136.

Lyotard, J.F. (1979) *The Postmodern Condition: A Report on Knowledge*. Minneapolis, MN: University of Minnesota Press.

Nutbrown, C. (2011) A box of childhood: small stories at the roots of a career. *International Journal of Early Years Education*, 19(3–4): 233–248.

References

Brookfield, S. (1995) *Becoming a Critically Reflective Teacher*. San Francisco, CA: Jossey-Bass.

Chatham House (2002) *Chatham House Rule*. Available at: www.chatham-house.org/chatham-house-rule-faq (accessed 15 March 2019).

Christie, D. and Viner, R. (2005) ABC of adolescence: adolescent development. *BMJ*, 330(7486): 301–304.

Clark-Keefe, K. (2009) Between antagonism and surrender: using art to dwell more resolutely in irresolution. *Creative Approaches to Research*, 2(1): 22–35.

Cohen, L., Mannion, L. and Morrison, K. (2011) *Research Methods in Education*, 7th edn. London: RoutledgeFalmer.

Denzin, N. and Lincoln, Y. (2011) The discipline and practice of qualitative research. In N. Denzin and Y. Lincoln (eds), *The Sage Handbook of Qualitative Research*, 4th edn. Thousand Oaks CA: Sage, pp. 1–20.

Donaldson, M. (1978) *Children's Minds*. London: Fontana.

Ellis, C. (2004) *The Ethnographic I: A Methodological Novel about Autoethnography*. Walnut Creek, CA: AltaMira Press.

Gauntlett, D. (2007) *Creative Explorations: New Approaches to Identities and Audiences*. London: Routledge.

Gauntlett, D. and Awan, F. (2011) Action-based visual and creative methods in social research. In I. Heywood and B. Sandywell (eds), *The Handbook of Visual Culture*. Oxford: Berg.

Gee, P. (2000) Identity as an analytic lens for research in education. *Review of Research in Education*, 25: 99–125.

Kamberelis, G. and Dimitriadis, G. (2011) Focus groups. In N. Denzin and Y. Lincoln (eds), *The Sage Handbook of Qualitative Research*, 4th edn. London: Sage, pp. 835–850.

Kendall, A. and Perkins, H. (2014) *Creative Research Methods in a College-Based Higher Education Setting*. York: Higher Education Academy.

Kress, T.M. (2011) Stepping out of the academic brew: using critical research to break down hierarchies of knowledge production. *International Journal of Qualitative Studies in Education*, 24(3): 267–283.

Krueger, R. and Casey, M. (2015) *Focus Groups: A Practical Guide for Applied Research*, 5th edn. London: Sage.

Lyotard, J.F. (1979) *The Postmodern Condition: A Report on Knowledge.* Minneapolis, MN: University of Minnesota Press.

Merriam, S., Johnson-Bailey, J., Lee, M., Kee, Y., Ntseane, G. and Mazanah Muhamad, M. (2001) Power and positionality: negotiating insider/outsider status within and across cultures. *International Journal of Lifelong Education,* 20(5): 405–416.

Nutbrown, C. (2011) A box of childhood: small stories at the roots of a career. *International Journal of Early Years Education,* 19(3–4): 233–248.

Nutbrown, C. (2018) *Early Childhood Educational Research.* London: Sage.

Pahl, K. and Rowsell, J. (2010) *Artifactual Literacies: Every Object Tells a Story.* New York: Teachers College Press.

Perkins, H. (2017) *From Training to Qualification: The Journey of Level 3 Early Years Student Practitioners.* PhD thesis, University of Sheffield. Avaialble at: http://etheses.whiterose.ac.uk (accessed 6 March 2019).

Pink, S. (ed.) (2007) *Visual Interventions.* New York: Berghan Books.

Pink, S. (2012) *Doing Visual Ethnography.* Sage: London.

Punch, K. (2006) *Developing Effective Research Proposals.* London: Sage.

Sultana, F. (2007) Reflexivity, positionality and participatory ethics: negotiating fieldwork dilemmas in international research. *ACME: An International E-Journal for Critical Geographies,* 6(3): 374–385. Available at: www.acme-journal.org/vol6/FS.pdf (accessed 17 May 2012)

Wellington, J. (2000) *Educational Research.* London: Continuum.

Narrative inquiry

Storying lived experiences with early childhood student-practitioners

Lynn Richards

Introduction

This chapter offers an exploration of the methodological framework of narrative inquiry. This approach can accommodate a range of research methods, and the chapter will incorporate details of both photo- and metaphor-elicitation, as creative methods, as ways to enhance the quality of the gathered data. My doctoral study focused on students' engagement and sense of belonging within higher education, and is discussed within these pages to show how I used narrative inquiry to capture the voices of my research participants, who became the narrators of their stories (Chase, 2011). Researchers at levels 6 and 7 who wish to focus in similar ways on the privileging of participant voice may be attracted to narrative inquiry. Research is not always straightforward since the topics studied are often 'messy, complicated, uncertain, and soft' (Bochner, 2002: 258), so that a framework to encompass them fully can be challenging. In light of this, the chapter will identify a range of strengths and limitations that I experienced regarding narrative inquiry, together with methods of elicitation, that were revealed within the research study. The chapter will close with some thoughts on recommendations for future use of the research approach.

The research approach

Narrative inquiry foregrounds the voice of the participant to offer detailed responses to questions that, within the more traditional qualitative processes, have been suppressed and ultimately discarded as data not conforming to the questioning process (Mishler, 1986: 54). In narrative inquiry, the use of generative and open questions can offer participants the chance to tell their stories, to detail their experiences, and to dwell upon those aspects that they wish to convey to their listener. Even the simplest of questions then has the potential to be interpreted in its own way and to be responded to in ways that are framed by the participant (Paget, 1983). As a way to encourage lengthy contributions, the narrative inquirer becomes Holstein and Gubrium's (1995) 'active interviewer (who) does far more than dispassionate questioning; he or she *activates narrative production*' (p. 39, original emphasis); the participant is invited to view the research topic from a range of perspectives, by shifting 'narrative positions' (Holstein and Gubrium, 1995: 77), in order to explore the variety of meanings that might be held. One of my participants showed signs of missing her family, and so I shifted the conversation to her home life before having come to university; the participant quickly identified the sense of personal space and freedom that she valued living away from the familial home. Such an approach allows for a responsive process where design can be explored to work more actively with participants (Riessman, 1990).

The responsive nature of the methodology is a key feature. Reducing the power differential between the researcher and the participant seeks to establish an equal and respectful interaction wherein the participant is appreciated as one who is expert in their own life; that is, their knowledge and experience (Mishler, 1986) are affirmed within the research relationship. This has implications for the storytelling within the research process since the context of the relationship will influence what is told, and how it is told, inclusive of factors to do with researcher and participant characteristics, geographical location, and cultural/historical context. For example, Riessman (2008) details her research with South Asian women around childbirth practices and reflects upon her own white American status to make sense of what she is being told; the telling is further distanced in this case by the necessity of a translator. Differing cultural norms are recognised by Riessman (2008), who discusses the interpretive challenges; while she portrays 'Sunita' as a childless woman, it is one year later when she is contacted by Sunita to identify herself as a 'complete woman' (p. 42).

Narrative inquiry offers a means to 'story' lived experience, and yet language is not regarded as a transparent medium. Rather, the philosophical position is taken that 'language is deeply constitutive of reality, not simply a technical device for establishing meaning. Informants' stories do not mirror a world "out there". They are constructed creatively, authored, rhetorical, replete with assumptions, and interpretive' (Riessman, 1993: 4–5). Narrative inquirers, then, do not merely consider the 'what' that has been told, but scrutinise the 'how' of narrative construction in order to understand more fully (Elliott, 2005). The ability to tell a good story, to show oneself in a favourable light and to be understood by one's listener reflects what Riessman (1990) terms the 'teller's problem'; having been offered a topic, it is the participant who is tasked with retrieving memories of appropriate experiences in order to make sense of them in light of researcher questioning. As noted previously, differing cultural practices can act as a barrier to communication, both for the teller and the listener. The 'how' of the telling may be couched in false starts, non-lexicals (Riessman, 1990) such as 'uh-huh', hesitations, pauses and repetitions. For instance, in my study, an Asian Muslim narrator displays many false starts before finally declaring, 'basically, to the point . . . wearing the scarf is another thing that puts a barrier to . . . developing friendship relationships. That's . . . that's what I think' (Richards, 2018: 144).

The presence of such recorded details within the transcribed words can bring a sense of verisimilitude of the original occasion to the reader at a later time and reflect the inward struggle of the teller to compose a suitable story. As a way to facilitate a two-way exchange, meanings are co-constructed between researcher and participant during the research interaction so that it becomes the site of production of the narrative: 'a discourse between speakers . . . [in which] the meanings of questions and responses are contextually grounded and jointly constructed' (Mishler, 1986: 33–34). In this way, meanings can be clarified and understandings agreed at the time.

The truth of the stories told is not a particular concern within narrative inquiry (Chase, 2005; Riessman, 2008) since it is what the stories might tell the listener that is of significance; how the stories reflect the stance of the teller and how the experience has been understood by the teller. Inclusion of researcher 'utterances' (Mishler, 1999) within transcriptions can be helpful in seeing how 'shifts' in the narrative might have been affected, such as a question or interjection that redirects the flow of talk (Paget, 1983). An example drawn from my study is when I was affected by what I was being told: 'Sorry. I'm feeling really emotional. That sounds great . . . Oh dear (sniffs)' (Richards, 2018: 137). It was then I, as researcher, who was redirected by my narrator to the topic of belonging, which had not previously been mentioned on that occasion; I suspect my narrator was trying to get me back on track and so help me to resume my composure. Detailed transcriptions can assist in the dialogic aspects of the research activity, whereby readers too are invited into the recorded words to engage in the interpretive space. Such an invitation values the multivocality of a narrative text and acknowledges that the provision of ample research materials can afford the reader the chance to make a different interpretation from the one of the researcher, as well as conceding that future interpretations will be shaped by differing social realities (Gullestad, 1996, cited in Nielsen, 1999) and so challenge original understandings.

INDIVIDUAL/GROUP TASK

What skills and attributes do you have to offer within the narrative inquiry approach? What are your areas of strength and what might be areas for further improvement? And what might be your area(s) of vulnerability?

There is no one method of narrative analysis (Elliott, 2005; Riessman, 1993) so that considerable scope is given to the researcher to draw meaning from the stories gathered. The seminal work of Labov and Waletzky (1967) offers a structural analysis of the narrative, so highlighting the variety of functional clauses within it, although identifying this can be problematic in more extended narrative texts (Riessman, 1993). Riessman (1990) discusses, among other things, an analysis using four genres – story, habitual, hypothetical and episodic – and how these might be identified to give meaning to a text and so aid the interpretation. For instance, within my own research, one of my narrators often uses a 'habitual' genre, which I interpreted as reflecting the routine and dullness of her days on campus:

'We just go and sit in there and have some lunch . . . So I don't really see many people in there. It's just, we go in and get some food and then go back to our next lecture'. Narrative texts can also be analysed by the use of a more poetic format, using stanzas of narrators' words (Edwards, 2015; Etherington, 2007; Riessman, 1993) that are arranged in a way to aid the interpretation while also adding to the 'feel' of the text. I used poetic stanzas in my own study, and details are included later in this chapter.

Uses of the research approach within the early education sector

Narrative inquiry lends itself to extensive storying of experiences within the early education sector. In the realms of social work and health services, narrative research has been increasingly used to gather the experiences of those who live and work according to a particular policy context (Riessman and Quinney, 2005) and those who live with a particular health condition (Clark and Mishler, 1992). Within early childhood education, research might be done with, and for: practitioners, to more fully understand the challenges that exist in contemporary day-to-day working practices; parents, to appreciate the benefits and concerns they realise in using the service; and leaders and managers, to examine the current issues that impact the sector.

Early education has been subject to many reforms over the years and the policy context has necessarily impacted the lives of all concerned; that is, something has happened to change practice. The functional clauses of a structural analysis of narrative (Labov and Waletzky, 1967) identify those elements denoting a 'complicating action', a temporal component, of something having happened, and an 'evaluation', which provides the meaning of the events of the narrative for the listener (Elliott, 2005). The necessity to understand the meaning of behaviours and experiences offered within narrative research facilitates the quality of empathy (Elliott, 2005), since it requires the listener to appreciate the perspective of the narrator. This would seem a valuable means of working towards respectful and ethical practices in early education where the stakes are high; it is the well-being of very young children that is the focus of the sector.

INDIVIDUAL/GROUP TASK

Can you think of a policy context or change in practice that has had significant implications for the early childhood education sector? Who might you approach to gather stories about this change and what it means to them in practice? What might be the value of such narratives, and for whom?

In my doctoral research, my narrators were second-year undergraduates on either an early childhood studies degree or an early years primary teacher training degree. They storied their lived experiences of being on placement within the early education settings and having had to engage with a variety of organisational and managerial practices. 'Complicating actions' included being made to feel unwelcome in the staff room during the lunch break and having the opportunity to take two sets of 'lowers' (low-achiever groups) on a forest walk. The 'evaluation' of this latter event is reflected in the words of my narrator: 'Like, they aren't animals. They can get on with things . . . Nobody ran away. It was such a good lesson though, just having that freedom like' (Richards, 2018: 159). The narrative inquiry approach afforded this narrator the chance to talk at length, to decide upon which events to mention, and to offer a rich and detailed account of how she felt about the experience. Insights to do with the ability of the 'lowers', the quality of the learning on offer, and the lack of restraint or control are instructive, and reflect this narrator's storying of experience in light of an open question about how she experienced a sense of belonging in the placement setting. For her, the qualities of respect (from the teacher), choice (her negotiation to take two sets of 'lowers') and responsibility (she was trusted to be capable) combined to generate a sense of belonging, and the narrative inquiry methodology offered her scope for such ideas to be expressed on her own terms.

Use of the research approach within my study
Storying Students' Ecologies of Belonging: A Narrative Inquiry into the Relationship between 'First-Generation' Students and the University

I sought to uncover the meanings of my narrators' experiences, and I was heavily influenced by the work of Clandinin and Connelly (2000), whose narrative inquiry approach is based on Dewey's (1938/1997) principles of seeking to find meaning within experience and wherein the '*the person* in context is of prime interest' (Clandinin and Connelly, 2000: 32, original emphasis). Moving away from a schedule of questions, I wanted to be led by my participants, although I also realised that they may not readily find expression for such concepts, perhaps not having considered them previously. The need, then, to offer creative methods (Kara, 2015), to facilitate the focus upon participant-talk, drove the research design to incorporate elements of both photo- and metaphor-elicitation. These pictorial and figurative means of expression, used specifically within the third, and final, conversation to reveal narrators' articulations of belonging, sought to open up more conventional verbal processes; dialogue that could encompass meanings, and in turn meanings that could be co-constructed within the research interaction itself, which within narrative inquiry becomes the focus of study (Elliott, 2005; Mishler, 1986, 1999; Riessman, 1990, 1993).

Photo-elicitation can enhance the participatory nature of a research study by inviting participants to bring along photos that 'speak' to them of the topic in question: to express young people's ideas around teenage sexuality (Allen, 2011); to explore the experience of homelessness (Packard, 2008); and to examine the lives of black middle-class male youth (Allen, 2012). I asked my narrators to take, or acquire, photos that spoke to them of belonging in order that we could 'reveal its contours' (Allen, 2011: 501) within our co-constructed research interaction. For example, one narrator brought along a photo of a stone-encrusted ring; it belonged to her mother. Discussion of the photo revealed that the ring had been handed down to the women within the family through many generations, and that the ring would at some future point be passed to the narrator. Factors to do with tradition, cultural norms, family, gender, responsibility and status were encapsulated within this one photo of a ring, and the elicitation method provided a means to reveal such detail; the 'teller's problem' (Riessman, 1990), reflected within the construction of a suitable narrative, was aptly accommodated within the methodological framework of narrative inquiry.

Since my aim was to encourage my narrators to story their experience, speaking at length, I did not wish them to struggle to find the words necessary to explain their ideas. The work of Fletcher (2013) introduced me to the method of metaphor-elicitation, and reveals her 'fascination with the ebb and flow of verbal processes of meaning making and the role that these processes play in the formation and reformation of individual and shared understanding' (p. 1551). Metaphor, as a means to offer a picture in words, added to my creative strategies to enhance the narratives offered within my research. I invited narrators to think about what belonging might feel like, and then to describe it to me in terms of something else: 'If I were to ask you about student belonging, and to describe it as something else, what would you describe it as?' (Richards, 2018: 94). For one narrator, the metaphor of a lifeboat was realised, and, when questioned by me, in a question-and-answer-style format, she was able to offer quite explicit details to do with the boat:

> There's nobody sat at the top / Shouting orders as such / Yeah / We're all paddling together / Keeping the boat afloat you might say / Yeah / Helping each other to keep afloat / That's a good one / I like that / Yeah.
>
> (Richards, 2018: 130).

INDIVIDUAL/GROUP TASK

Inclusion is a prized quality of early education provision. How might you use photo- and/or metaphor-elicitation methods to explore the concept of inclusion with practitioners/parents/management?

My research study involved the participation of seven narrators, all women, and I worked with each one separately, talking with them in 'conversation' lasting one hour, on three occasions; our conversations were digitally recorded so that they could be transcribed for greater depth of analysis and interpretation. I also listened to the digital recordings while reading the transcripts so that I could begin to grasp the finer details to do with voice tone, inflection, and use of pauses (Riessman, 1993) to help with the interpretive process. I presented much of my research data as poetic stanzas, based on the 'parsing' of words according to Gee (1985), whereby oral aspects of the spoken word are privileged, and lines of text are determined by pitch and intonation rather than the function of a clause (Labov and Waletzky, 1967). As a result, I used the narrators' own words and arranged them in groups of lines – stanzas – to more effectively give a sense of the actual conversation, to draw in my reader, and to add to the analysis and interpretation of the text. As an example of such 'fusion of form and content' (Mishler, 1999: 20), I offer data presented as stanzas when one of my narrators responds to a question about how a sense of belonging might be established within a school classroom:

> I don't let people know when I'm struggling
> So I just get on with it
> I just keep myself to myself
>
> Some placements will just refer to you as the student
> And not give you an actual name
> And it's kind of annoying
> What can you do?
>
> If you see a particular shy child
> Make sure you engage with them
> Because they are not going to engage with you
> So you need to make that effort to talk to them
>
> Because I was the shy one in school
> I just kind of kept myself to myself
> I just keep myself to myself
>
> And just get on with everything
> I'm quite shy and quiet
> People can think I'm rude
> But I'm just quiet
>
> Like if you see a shy child
> Just like engage with them
> Because they will feel more secure and wanted and valued

So yeah
Just notice everyone
Because you will always have the shy kids at the back
That's who you need to engage with
(Richards, 2018: 127–128)

Perspectives on the strengths and limitations of the research approach and some thoughts on recommendations for its future use

My choice of narrative inquiry for my doctoral study was based upon the interplay of my own lived experience, my values, and my professional training. Having worked with young people and adult learners in an informal way for over two decades, I was drawn to a methodology where the voice of the research participant was to be privileged and where I could use active listening skills. As a university lecturer, I have used a wide repertoire of creative teaching/learning strategies – role play, drawings, simulations, debates, posters – so that I felt comfortable with the possibilities offered by creative methods to do with photo- and metaphor-elicitation. It was important for me that I employed methods that suited both my aims and my own value base. Having declared such a positioning, I outline below what I consider to be some of the many strengths and limitations of the methods discussed within this chapter; referenced materials are designed to signal avenues for further reading.

Strengths

- Voices of participants are privileged, and 'through creative media voices are made free in their space' (Finnigan, 2009: 148).

- Respectful and empathic listening to the narrator affords the chance for the potentiality of the individual to be revealed (Rogers, 1990: 30).

- Large extracts of text that are not 'fractured' (Riessman, 1993), as in more traditional qualitative data presentation, can add to the integrity of the narrator's voice.

■ Talking at length within research contexts can offer the opportunity for meaning-making and so provide a therapeutic outcome for the narrator (Elliott, 2005).

■ Narrative inquiry offers the chance to work collaboratively with narrators within the analysis and interpretation stages via the use of 'research interim texts' (Clandinin and Connelly, 2000: 133), where negotiation of shared understandings, as part of an iterative process, can add to the authenticity of final research texts.

■ Metaphor offers a way 'to conceptualise one thing in terms of something else that we understand more readily' (Lakoff and Johnson, 2003: 61).

Limitations

■ Creative strategies require the researcher and the participant to work with uncertainty owing to the open-ended nature of the outcomes (Kara, 2015).

■ Large extracts of text can compromise narrator anonymity and confidentiality, whereby detailed accounts can reveal the identity of the person telling the story (Riessman, 2008).

■ The inclusion of narrators' photos could have added to the visual appeal of my research study, but the potential for harm to narrators (BERA, 2011) was considered too risky. The question of who owned the photos would also have required lengthy ethical consideration since photos were generally offered on mobile phones.

■ Metaphors may be experienced differently within differing cultural and linguistic norms (Lakoff and Johnson, 2003) so that understandings need to be clarified between researcher and narrator.

The significance of the early education sector for the well-being of our future generations is irrefutable. And yet many early childhood practitioners are still not financially remunerated to reflect their worth to our children. I would argue, then, that the voices of all those involved in early education need to be heard in order to move the hearts and minds of those who have the authority to review funding streams and ameliorate working conditions. Narrative inquiry is a way to privilege the voice of the participant, who becomes the narrator of stories, as a means to generate knowledge for both epistemological and political reasons: 'those systematically excluded from knowledge generation need to be active participants in the research process, especially when it is about them' (Brydon-Miller et al., 2011: 389).

Summary

- Narrative inquiry foregrounds the voice of the participant.

- Meaning is co-constructed within the context of the research interaction.

- Creative methods can be incorporated to facilitate expression of ideas both within the gathering of stories and in the analysis and interpretation processes.

Recommended reading

Paget, M.A. (1983) Experience and knowledge. *Human Studies*, 6: 67–90.
Polkinghorne, D.E. (2007) Validity issues in narrative research. *Qualitative Inquiry*, 13(4): 471–486.
Riessman, C.K. (1990) *Divorce Talk: Women and Men Make Sense of Personal Relationships*. New Brunswick. NJ: Rutgers University Press.

References

Allen, L. (2011) 'Picture this': using photo-methods in research on sexualities and schooling. *Qualitative Research*, 11(5): 487–504.
Allen, Q. (2012) Photographs and stories: ethics, benefits and dilemmas using participant photography with black middle-class youth. *Qualitative Research*, 12(4): 443–458.
Bochner, A.P. (2002) Criteria against ourselves. In N.K. Denzin and Y.S. Lincoln (eds), *The Qualitative Inquiry Reader*. London: Sage, pp. 257–265.
British Education Research Association (BERA) (2011) *Ethical Guidelines of Educational Research*. London: BERA. Available at: www.bera.ac.uk/wp-content/uploads/2014/02/BERA-Ethical-Guidelines-2011.pdf?noredirect=1 (accessed 4 November 2017).

Brydon-Miller, M., Kral, M., Maguire, P., Noffke, S. and Sabhlok, A. (2011) Jazz and the banyan tree: roots and riffs on participatory action research. In N.K. Denzin and Y.S. Lincoln (eds), *The Sage Handbook of Qualitative Research*, 4th edn. London: Sage, pp. 387–400.

Chase, S.E. (2005) Narrative inquiry: multiple lenses, approaches, voices. In N.K. Denzin and Y.S. Lincoln (eds), *The Sage Handbook of Qualitative Research*, 3rd edn. London: Sage, pp. 651–680.

Chase, S.E. (2011) Narrative inquiry: still a field in the making. In N.K. Denzin and Y.S. Lincoln (eds), *The Sage Handbook of Qualitative Research*, 4th edn. London: Sage, pp. 421–434.

Clandinin, D.J. and Connelly, F.M. (2000) *Narrative Inquiry: Experience and Story in Qualitative Research*. San Francisco, CA: Jossey-Bass.

Clark, J.A. and Mishler, E.G. (1992) Attending to patients' stories: reframing the clinical task. *Sociology of Health and Illness*, 14(3): 344–372.

Dewey, J. (1938/1997) *John Dewey: Experience and Education*. New York: Simon & Schuster.

Edwards, S. (2015) Transforming the findings of narrative research into poetry. *Nurse Researcher*, 22(5): 35–39.

Elliott, J. (2005) *Using Narrative in Social Research: Qualitative and Quantitative Approaches*. London: Sage.

Etherington, K. (2007) Ethical research in reflexive relationships. *Qualitative Inquiry*, 13(5): 599–616.

Finnigan, T. (2009) 'Tell us about it': diverse student voices in creative practice. *Art, Design & Communication in Higher Education*, 8(2): 135–150.

Fletcher, G. (2013) Of baby ducklings and clay pots: method and metaphor in HIV prevention. *Qualitative Health Research*, 23(11): 1551–1562.

Gee, J.P. (1985) The narrativization of experience in the oral style. *Journal of Education*, 167: 9–35.

Holstein, J.A. and Gubrium, J.F. (1995) *The Active Interview*. London: Sage.

Kara, H. (2015) *Creative Research Methods in the Social Sciences: A Practical Guide*. Bristol: Policy Press.

Labov, W. and Waletzky, J. (1967) *Narrative Analysis: Oral Version of Personal Experience*. From: American Ethnological Soc: Proc 1966 Annual Spring Meeting: 'Essays on the Verbal and Visual Arts'. Washington: UP.

Lakoff, G. and Johnson, M. (2003) *Metaphors We Live By*. Chicago, IL: University of Chicago Press.

Mishler, E.G. (1986) *Research Interviewing: Context and Narrative*. Cambridge, MA: Harvard University Press.

Mishler, E.G. (1999) *Storylines: Craftartists' Narratives of Identity*. Cambridge, MA: Harvard University Press.

Nielsen, H.B (1999) 'Black holes' as sites for self-constructions. In R. Josselson and A. Lieblich (eds), *Making Meaning of Narratives*. London: Sage, pp. 45–75.

Packard, J. (2008) 'I'm gonna show you what it's really like out here': the power and limitation of participatory visual methods. *Visual Studies*, 23(1): 63–77.

Paget, M.A. (1983) Experience and knowledge. *Human Studies*, 6: 67–90.

Richards, L. (2018) *Storying Students' Ecologies of Belonging: A Narrative Inquiry into the Relationship between 'First Generation' Students and the University*. Unpublished EdD thesis, University of Wolverhampton.

Riessman, C.K. (1990) *Divorce Talk: Women and Men Make Sense of Personal Relationships*. New Brunswick, NJ: Rutgers University Press.

Riessman, C.K. (1993) *Narrative Analysis*. London: Sage.

Riessman, C.K. (2008) *Narrative Methods for the Human Sciences*. London: Sage.

Riessman, C.K. and Quinney, L. (2005) Narrative in social work: a critical review. *Qualitative Social Work*, 4(4): 391–412.

Rogers, C. (1990) Client-centred therapy. In H. Kirschenbaum and V.L. Henderson (eds), *Carl Rogers Dialogues: Conversations with Martin Buber, Paul Tillich, B.F. Skinner, Gregory Bateson, Michael Polyani, Rollo May, and Others*. London: Constable, pp. 9–38.

The use of observations in early childhood research

Jackie Musgrave

Introduction

The aim of this chapter is to describe and evaluate the use of child-hood observations as a tool for educational research. While the focus of the chapter is educational research, the content can be applied to how observations can be used in early years practice (Rose and Rogers, 2012). The chapter starts with an overview of how observations have been used historically by the pioneers who have helped us to learn about children's learning and development. I will draw on how I used observations as a tool for my doctoral research, which explored how practitioners create inclusive environments for young children with chronic health conditions. The ethical considerations that need to be considered in relation to observing young children will be discussed in detail.

Definition of observation

The Oxford English Dictionary (2018) defines 'observations' as 'the action or careful process of closely observing or monitoring something or someone'. The use of observations is embedded in early childhood practice and is a key aspect of assessment. In England, the Early Years Foundation Stage (DfE, 2017) statutory guidance for the standards of care and education for children aged 0–5 years old requires practitioners to carry out observations of children in order to assess their learning needs. The focus of this chapter discusses observations as a research tool.

Historical perspective

Early childhood education is a relatively new field of academia, and being a researcher and making a contribution to knowledge is an exciting and privileged place to be. However, it is important that we acknowledge and look back at the legacy of the theorists and pioneers who have laid the foundations for early years practitioners to follow. We owe a debt of gratitude to the educators, doctors, developmental psychologist and philosophers who laid the foundations and have helped us to build the body of knowledge about children's learning and development. One of the research methods that many of the people who went before us used was the tool of observation.

When observations have been used appropriately

The origins of systematic observations to enable understanding of how children develop can be traced to Charles Darwin in the middle of the nineteenth century. He not only observed animal behaviour, but he also compiled and kept meticulous journals that recorded the day-to-day observations of the behaviour of his eldest son. Moving into the first couple of decades of the twentieth century, Jean Piaget is possibly the most famous researcher in the field of children's development. He observed young children extensively, most notably his own three children, Laurent, Lucienne and Jacqueline, using his findings to inform his theories of child development. Halfpenny and Pettersen (2014) claim that the strength of Piaget's work and the theories that he developed are a consequence of what they describe as 'his approach to learning based on very detailed, practical precise and attentive observation of young children' (p. 10). Thinking of this in a contemporary context, it may seem improbable to base a life's work on predominantly one's own children; however it is important to bear in mind that Piaget was a pioneer in the field of cognitive development. In addition, as I will explain below, my knowledge and understanding of inclusive practice was informed by using observations on just one child.

A contemporary of Piaget's was Susan Isaacs, who was a pioneer of nursery education in England almost 100 years ago. In a similar way to Piaget, Isaacs carried out detailed observations on children; her diary entries contain ongoing observations of children's conversations about concepts such as life and death. She famously wrote about the children's fascination with the nursery's pet rabbit who had died. In order to help the children understand what had happened to the rabbit, she allowed them to dig up the rabbit's body to see if he was still dead. She included reflections on her observations and wrote to Piaget to discuss their views on children's development. Accounts of her views on early childhood education are peppered with how she used observations to create her pedagogical approach to the teaching of children (Nutbrown et al., 2012).

When observations have been used inappropriately

In the middle of the last century, Arnold Gessell, a developmental psychologist who has informed our knowledge of children's physical, social and intellectual development, used observations in his research. In order to do so, Gessell created a giant dome that became known as a test tube because of the scientific research that was conducted there. It shows the researchers carrying out observations; there is a cot that was placed in the middle of the 'test tube' with a baby, dressed in just a nappy, sitting in the cot. It reveals an electric spotlight that is focused on the baby, and the figure of a man dressed in a white coat and holding a clipboard and pen can be seen. Imagine the feelings such an experience could have provoked in the babies and young children who were the focus of his research, undressed and separated from their main carers in an alien and unnatural environment. Clearly, such an approach to conducting research would be regarded as unethical in contemporary research; examining the use of observations in research from the past helps to remind us why there is a need to invest time and thought to ethical permissions and considerations.

Mary Ainsworth, a developmental psychologist, used observations in her 'Strange Situation' research to examine the emotional relationship between babies and their primary caregivers (Ainsworth et al., 1978). The analysis of the observations of babies and caregivers helped

Ainsworth to develop her contribution to attachment theory. Watching films of the recordings of Ainsworth's experiments clearly shows the distress of the babies when they are separated from their caregiver. This influential and often quoted experiment is another example of how observations were used in ways that would be regarded as unethical for contemporary researchers.

Ethical considerations when using observations in early childhood research

Ethics is related to the moral responsibility we share as researchers to prevent harm to our participants. The historical background to the use of observations as a research tool in some of the research that is well known, and in many cases remains influential, highlights why there is a great deal of attention given to considering the ethics of research. Returning to Ainsworth's 'Strange Situation' observations, watching film footage helps to highlight some of the unethical aspects of the research. For example, the baby in the film is deeply distressed when the mother leaves the room. The ethical considerations in relation to my research are explored in detail below.

Methods of observation

There are a number of observation methods that can be used in research. In brief, the methods include narrative, target child, time samples and checklists. Mukherji and Albon (2018) have a chapter that gives a useful introduction to the use of observations in educational research. For my research, I adapted the approach used in the Effective Early Learning (EEL) Project developed by Bertram and Pascal (2006) combined as an observation tool. The following section explains the context of my research and includes justifications for selecting observations, and specifically why I used the BEEL approach as a way of observing a child for my research. The strengths and limitations of observations as a research method will also be discussed.

> **INDIVIDUAL/GROUP TASK**
>
> 1. Familiarise yourself with the different methods of observation.
>
> 2. Identify the ethical considerations in relation to observing children.

Research focus

I trained as a Registered Sick Children's Nurse and I have worked as a paediatric asthma nurse specialist, where I developed a deep interest in the care of children with asthma as well as other contemporary medical conditions. The presence of chronic conditions can have a profound impact on children's lives. For example, children with asthma can have their symptoms provoked by coming into contact with substances that can trigger an attack. Common triggers include animals, cold weather, pollen and emotions such as excitement. After I became an early years lecturer, I taught a health module to Foundation Degree students, and as I worked with the students they taught me how they adapted the child's environment in their early years settings in order to maximise their inclusion. A search of the education databases revealed that there was a dearth of research that looked at how chronic health conditions affected young children in their early education settings. Having identified a gap in our knowledge, I decided that my research question was: *How do practitioners create inclusive environments for young children with chronic health conditions?* I wanted to find out how practitioners adapted the environment for children with chronic health conditions. For example, I was keen to find out if the symptoms of eczema affect a young child's inclusion in messy or sensory play activities. Fargas-Malet et al. (2010) assert that observations have a long tradition as a method of researching young children's lives, and I felt that observing a child in his or her naturalistic environment was going to be the most effective way of exploring the child's perspective in relation to my research question. The observer can use their senses to absorb the events occurring in the child's environment and can use their body as a conduit to make connections between what is being seen and the theory or meaning that underlies the actions. The use of observations can be for the greater good of promoting knowledge about children.

In the context of this research, such an aim aligned with the aims of ethnographers, who strive, according to Angrosino (2005), through their research, which primarily uses observation methods, to advocate and be a spokesperson for a cause or issue. This aim linked back to Kate's, who is DJ's mum, wish that researching the effect of chronic health conditions on children would highlight the difficulties and effect on children in their early education setting.

Identifying a child to observe

Because of events that can only be described as serendipitous, I was helped in identifying a child to observe by his mum, who worked as a practitioner at the setting where I was conducting my research. 'Kate' was keen to help me with my research because she 'wanted there to be greater awareness of the ways that asthma, eczema and allergy to a range of foods, affected her son's life in order to help him and other children who also had a chronic health condition'. Her son, who became known as 'DJ', was 20 months old when I started the year-long period of observing him. Bronfenbrenner's (1994) ecological system theory is a useful theory to adopt in order to consider the contexts of children's lives. The innermost context, or 'microsystem', is the one where children spend most of their lives, and this is usually the child's home. However, McDowall-Clark (2013) reminds us that many children spend a significant amount of their lives in the microsystem of an early childhood setting; consequently, she adapted Bronfenbrenner's theory and points out that many children have two microsystems (i.e. their home and early childhood setting). Therefore, using observations as a research tool was helpful to collect global data about DJ and gain a snapshot of his life in his early years microsystem. I especially wanted to note DJ's choices of play activities, as well as finding out what meal times were like for him, and to note if the symptoms of his chronic conditions were evident. In particular, I wanted to note if he scratched the eczematous patches, which may indicate that he was experiencing discomfort. Having been given the privilege of permission to observe DJ, the next decision was to decide how to observe him in order to capture data that would help me to answer my research question.

Ethical considerations for observing DJ

As part of the planning for my research, I completed the university's research ethics application. This regulatory process is an essential aspect of the research process; however, it is vital that ethics are considered at every step of the process, and not just seen as a regulatory necessity. The need to consider ethics has become paramount in order to minimise any harm to participants as a consequence of research activity. Ensuring the anonymity of the child is a given, and, as I explained to DJ's mum, in order to protect his identity (and the setting's), her son would be given a pseudonym rather than use his real name. I asked her how she would like me to refer to her son. She said that she would like to discuss this with her family and that she would let me know what they decided. A few days later, she emailed me to inform me that the family would like him to be referred to as 'DJ' because they were the initials of his two grandfathers. The careful consideration given by DJ's mum in selecting his pseudonym indicated that this was important to her and his family. It supported Flewitt's (2005) suggestion that encouraging participants to select pseudonyms can help to impart a sense of control to the participants. However, I would offer that in my research, including Kate in the choice of pseudonym appeared to make her feel involved, and perhaps gave her a sense of involvement in the research that was being conducted with her son as a participant.

Selecting an observation tool

I was familiar with the range of observation methods available, (Riddall-Leech, 2008), but I was not sure of the approach that would be the right one for the aim of my observations of DJ. In order to inform my decision about which technique to use, I made a familiarisation visit to the toddler room in order to consider my position in the room as researcher. I was aiming to ensure that my presence would create minimal disruption to the usual running of the room. However, during my visit, many of the other children were deeply interested in my presence and were keen to interact with me. This had implications for the choice of observation method to be used. I could not adopt an approach that meant I was focused solely on DJ because I would not be able not able to acknowledge and interact with other children. Therefore, a narrative approach for lengthy periods of time was not going to be suitable. The approach used in the aforementioned EEL Project (Bertram and Pascal, 2006) has short and sharp periods of observations and avoids long narrative. Therefore, I elected to observe DJ for five minutes every 20 minutes. To capture the data, I used a recording sheet on which to scribble notes for each series of observations (see Figure 13.1). The date and times were recorded and kept in order to add to the audit trail of data collected in my research.

Using this adapted EEL method gave me a clear and consistent approach to the observations. I was able to gain an overall view of DJ's life in his setting throughout a sustained period of time. The use of observations in this way was a way of shining a torchlight on DJ, as well as giving me the broader context of his setting.

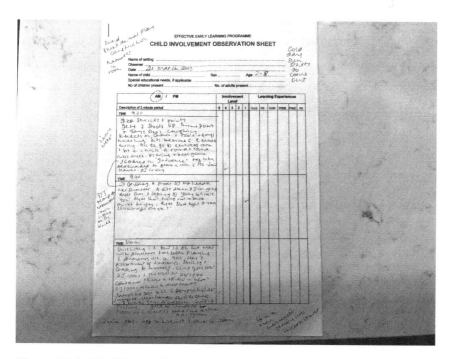

Figure 13.1 The Effective Early Learning (EEL) Child Involvement Observation Sheet

Source: Bertram and Pascal (2006)

Reflections from my research

This section includes notes from my research journal, where I wrote about the ethical considerations I identified in relation to observing DJ, which included:

- confidentiality;

- anonymity;

- consent – parent and child;

- interpreting the voice of the child;

- consideration of other children;

- consideration of other practitioners; and

- safeguarding.

Part of the ethical or moral considerations I was conscious of was that I had a responsibility to the children, the parents and the practitioners, all who were trusting me to go into the setting, but most of all I had a sense of responsibility to DJ. How was I going to interpret what I saw and speak for him? These are dilemmas about using observations for research, and may not be applicable to the use of observations that are conducted by practitioners for assessment purposes who are familiar to the child. I was cautious about swooping in and making a relationship with him because I was not going to be there to continue a relationship. Equally, I did not want to be aloof and watchful, possibly making him and the staff feel uncomfortable, I did not want them to feel as if they were under the microscope. So, the balance I struck was that I would be in the room and help out in small ways to try to blend in; however, I am aware that inevitably my presence would have changed the dynamics of the room. Interpreting DJ's voice meant that I had to be meticulous about what I recorded, and I was constantly concerned that what I was seeing and recording was reliable, which is something we need to constantly remind ourselves about when observing children. I am very aware of the difference between doing observations when you have the privileged position of being a guest in a setting, and conducting research and being a practitioner in a busy early years setting – with several key children.

Observations of DJ

I visited DJ's setting on eight days to carry out observations over the course of a year. It was important to observe him indoors and outdoors, and during different weather and climate, to analyse how the environment he was in affected his participation in his early education. Figures 13.2 and 13.3 include the notes from the observations, and the text in italics are reflections made in my research journal.

INDIVIDUAL TASK

1. How could observations of a child or a group of children strengthen your research?

2. What are the limitations of using observations in educational research?

30th March, 1205 hrs: lunch time. There are 12 children sitting around two tables, waiting for their bowl containing lunch. Chilli con carne is served in a variety of different coloured bowls. As the bowls are put in front of each child, DJ gazes at the contents of each bowl. A bowl covered in cling film with his name on it is unwrapped and put in front of him. "Here you go DJ, here's your dinner" (practitioner). The food is brown rather than the red coloured food in the other children's bowls. He gazes at his bowl and then looks again at the other bowls of food and his gaze follows the children's hands as they put spoons of the food into their mouths. A practitioner says "Come on DJ, eat your dinner". DJ shakes his head. The practitioner picked up his spoon and pretends to eat the food: "yum, yum, now your turn DJ". DJ starts to feed himself.

My reflection: I have reflected on the use of the word 'gaze' in this observation and realise I selected it because DJ was not simply looking, but he was looking "steadily or intently, especially in thought" (Oxford English Dictionary). As well as gazing, DJ sat quietly, with his back erect and he fixed his gaze for a sustained period of time, watching intently and unsmilingly. The use of the word 'look', as opposed to gaze, demonstrates a less intensive scrutiny by DJ. DJ is an observer and his responses suggest he is beginning to understand that meal times are different for him (Research Journal entry 2nd April)

Figure 13.2 Observation 1: lunchtime

1450 hrs: The 'orange incident' snack time – children are called to the table. A brightly coloured bowl containing orange quarters still in their skins is put in the middle of the table. The room smells of oranges and the spring sun is shining on the oranges and they are glistening. DJ is gazing at the oranges, as the children are invited to help themselves. DJ looks with interest at the children sucking on the oranges. DJ and another boy are given a bread stick by a practitioner "Oranges aren't for you DJ and Josh". DJ gazes at the bread stick and then turns his gaze to a child eating a piece of orange, he repeats this action but looks at a different child each time.

1505 hrs: the children are still sitting at the table. DJ is given another breadstick. DJ points at the bowl, then his hand slowly goes towards the bowl, he puts his fingers on the edge of the bowl and a practitioner says "No DJ". He removes his hand but then repeats the action and sits for about 30 seconds with his hand on the bowl, his gaze alternates between looking at the breadstick and the orange segments. He takes small nibbles at the breadstick. He then slowly tries to move the bowl closer to him... a child is having his hands wiped and is told he can leave the table. DJ looks at the child who is toddling to the outdoor area. DJ makes a small sound, puts his half-eaten breadstick on the table, and leaves the table, he runs to the door and returns to the outdoor play area.

My reflection: *The 'orange incident' haunts me. He is 20 months old and he is clearly noticing difference between the food that he is given and other children's food. What is he thinking? His level of 'stillness' is striking for such a young child. His attention from the events of 'the orange incident' was only taken away when he realised he could leave the table and go outdoors. He sits and gazes and is still and silent, clearly thinking deeply. The routines for meal times are lengthy and I am wondering if this makes mealtimes difficult for DJ? Perhaps a snack station would be better in order to avoid prolonged periods of time sitting at a table?*

Many months later when writing up my thesis, I reflected again on DJ's body language and wondered if his head nods were significant. He did frequent nods of his head when he given the same food as the other children. Did his body language demonstrate that he was pleased that he was given the same food; he smiled during when given the same type of food. Did being given the same food make him feel the same as the other children and did this increase his sense of belonging? If so, this sense of being the same was important to DJ: even though he was so young, he was aware of difference about his food. The observations as a research tool gave me insight into 'DJ's' life in his setting.

Figure 13.3 Observation 2: the use of observations as a research tool gave me insight into DJ's life in his setting

Observations as a research tool

The use of observations as a research tool originated from scientific, positivist and quantitative research. This is a paradigm where reliable and repeatable methods and subjective findings are regarded as essential to support the validity and trustworthiness of research. The usefulness of observations as a tool in relation to researching children is illustrated in the examples of Piaget, Isaacs and Gessell's work described above. The use of observations in qualitative, interpretivist research was frequently employed in the field of anthropology, a discipline that uses ethnographic approaches. Ethnographers, 'ethno' meaning folk, research human societies, their cultures and how such cultures develop. Therefore, observations are a key tool for ethnographers. The use of observations in ethnography is associated with researchers who 'seek to construct explanatory frameworks, only after careful analysis of objectively recorded data' (Angrosino, 2005: 730). Clark and Moss (2011) advocate the use of observations as a piece of their mosaic approach in order to watch how children spend their time in a setting. In turn, the art of watching can be used to listen to the voice of the child in order to find out what it is like for a child in their setting. Similarly, Pascal and Bertram (2012) assert that the use of observations are key to understanding the experiences of children in day care.

Strengths and limitations of observations in research

Reflecting on the use of observations as a research tool, I realise that such was the strength of this method, it was the only tool that afforded me the rich data that helped me to learn about DJ and to observe how important it was for him to have the same food as the other children. Analysis of the observations helped me appreciate that he was being excluded from enjoying his food because of being served food that was different. The implications of this exclusive practice are unknown but require attention. So, in a similar way to Piaget, my findings were based on an even smaller sample of children than his, but the learning I gleaned from them was powerful. However, the approach I developed to observing DJ required me to be acutely aware of the impact my presence in the setting may have had on him, other children and the practitioners. In addition, using observations in my research meant that I was required to devote a great deal of time to what was only one of several other data collection methods that I used. In addition to observations, I used a postal survey, semi-structured interviews with practitioners and parents, and a questionnaire to parents.

Summary

■ Observations can be a powerful research tool.

■ Choosing the most suitable method of observation for your research requires careful thought.

■ The ethical considerations relating to observing children must include the perspectives of the child(ren), other children, practitioners and the researcher.

■ Careful analysis and critical reflection of the data collected is important to do as soon as possible; however, the passage of time can reveal further findings.

Suggested viewing

The Strange Situation – Mary Ainsworth, available at: www.youtube.com/ watch?v=QTsewNrHUHU (accessed 6 March 2019).

Recommended reading

Mukherji, P. and Albon, D. (2018) *Research Methods in Early Childhood: An Introductory Guide*. London: Sage.
Riddall-Leech, S (2008) *How to Observe Children*, 2nd edn. Harlow: Heinemann.

References

Ainsworth, M., Blehar, M., Waters, E. and Wall, S. (1978) *Patterns of Attachment*. Hillsdale, NJ: Erlbaum.
Angrosino, M.V. (2005) Recontextualizing observation: ethnography, pedagogy, and the prospects for a progressive political agenda. In N.K. Denzin and

Y.S. Lincoln (eds), *The Sage Handbook of Qualitative Research*. Thousand Oaks, CA: Sage, pp. 729–745.

Bertram, T. and Pascal, C. (2006) *The Effective Early Learning Project*. Birmingham: Amber Publications.

Bronfenbrenner, U. (1994) Ecological models of human development. In *International Encyclopaedia of Education*, vol. 3, 2nd edn. Oxford: Elsevier Sciences, pp. 1643–1647.

Clark, A. and Moss, P. (2011) *Listening to Young Children: The Mosaic Approach*, 2nd edn. London: NCB.

Department for Education (DfE) (2017) *Statutory Framework for the Early Years Foundation Stage: Setting the Standards for Learning, Development and Care for Children from Birth to Five*. Available at: www.foundationyears.org. uk/files/2017/03/EYFS_STATUTORY_FRAMEWORK_2017.pdf (accessed 6 January 2019).

Fargas-Malet, M., McSherry, D., Larkin, E. and Robinson, C. (2010) Research with children: methodological issues and innovative techniques. *Journal of Early Childhood Research*, 8(2): 175–191.

Flewitt, R. (2005) Conducting research with young children: some ethical considerations. *Early Child Development and Care*, 175(6): 553–565.

Halfpenny, A.M. and Pettersen, J. (2014) *Introducing Piaget: A Guide for Practitioners and Students in Early Years Education*. London: Routledge.

McDowall-Clark, R. (2013) *Childhood in Society for the Early Years*, 2nd edn. London: Sage/Learning Matters.

Mukherji, P. and Albon, D. (2018) *Research Methods in Early Childhood: An Introductory Guide*. London: Sage.

Musgrave, J. (2014) *How Do Practitioners Create Inclusive Environments for Children with Chronic Health Conditions? An Exploratory Case Study*. PhD thesis, University of Sheffield. Available at: http://etheses.whiterose.ac.uk/6174/1/ Jackie%20Musgrave%20-%20Final%20Thesis%20incl%20Access%20 Form%20for%20submission%2019-5-14.pdf (accessed 6 March 2019).

Nutbrown, C., Clough, P. and Selbie, P. (2012) *Early Childhood Education: History, Philosophy and Experience*. London: Sage.

Oxford English Dictionary (2018) *Observation*. Available at: https://en. oxforddictionaries.com/definition/observation (accessed 22 August 2018).

Pascal, C. and Bertram, T. (2012) Praxis, ethics and power: developing praxeology as a participatory paradigm for early childhood research. *European Early Childhood Education Research Journal*, 20(4): 477–492.

Riddall-Leech, S (2008) *How to Observe Children*, 2nd edn. Harlow: Heinemann.

Rose, J. and Rogers, S. (2012) *The Role of the Adult in Early Years Settings*. Maidenhead: Open University Press.

Q-methodology

Seeking communalities in perspectives of young children and practitioners

Zeta Brown and Gavin Rhoades

Introduction

Q-methodology (Q) is a robust and useful tool for researchers wishing to combine quantitative and qualitative data collection approaches in their research. The chapter begins with a consideration of Q as a full methodology, and the importance of a researcher's positionality for how they deploy Q and interpret the data produced. Some different projects where Q has been used are examined to illustrate some of its features and flexibilities. The process of how to effectively conduct Q-sorts with young participants is discussed. The chapter finishes with a summary and some recommended reading.

This chapter focuses on the ways Q can be used, particularly with younger participants in mind, and as such only provides an overview of the numerous steps involved in conducting a Q-methodology study. Rhoades and Brown (2019) provide a more detailed description of how to perform a full Q-methodology study aimed at beginning Q researchers.

Stephenson, Q as a methodology and the 'science of subjectivity'

It would be inaccurate to consider Q-methodology as merely a research or data collection method. It is in fact a methodology, and as such it is a way of thinking about research. William Stephenson invented Q-methodology in the 1930s and considered Q to be a new concept where scientists (originally in psychology) needed to think from a different perspective and embrace change. Q illustrated an interpretive twist on a research base that was focused on positivism (Goldman, 1999).

INDIVIDUAL/GROUP TASK

Before you continue with the chapter, we would recommend you briefly research the difference between interpretivist and positivist research. Can you define the difference between these research paradigms? Which paradigm is usually associated with qualitative (participants' perspectives) and quantitative (statistics/numerical data) research?

The positivist paradigm is aligned with the perspective that social reality is external to the individuals within it, and therefore imposed upon them. In linking the social and natural world, it searches for an objective reality out in society. It consequently continues to be highly regarded in natural science research as it has the potential to inform future policy, producing findings that can be generalisable (Cohen et al., 2007).

In contrast, the interpretivist paradigm endeavours to engage with the positions of the individuals being researched (Basit, 2010). Stephenson was concerned about the dominant positivist methods used in psychology and wanted to change the way participants were viewed (Watts and Stenner, 2012). He believed that there was a need to allow for subjectivity whereby participants could conduct the measurements, instead of being subjected to measurement (Brown, 1994–1995). This became known as the 'science of subjectivity'. This does not mean, however, that Stephenson was an interpretivist researcher. His work bridged the gap between positivist and post-positivist research rather than committing fully to what is currently regarded as interpretivism (Brown, 1997). He invented a methodology that appreciated the benefits of investigating the complexity in participants' perspectives using subjectivity in psychology research.

Many qualitative Q researchers, including interpretivists, are influenced by the work of Steven Brown, who states that differences in the use of Q show the flexibility within the methodology (Brown, 1991–1992). Brown's interest in political science takes the notion of Q outside its primary focus on psychology. Brown (1997) highlights a growing generation of researchers in psychology, health and social sciences who are embracing Q, owing to the subjective nature of the methodology, because they are interested in 'more than life measured by the pound' (Brown, 1996: 1). Brown argues that qualitative researchers can use Q without having either to set aside their principal approach or to engage in a simplistic welding together of quantitative and qualitative methods.

There are Q characteristics that are seen in most Q studies. These include the consideration of subjectivity, the concourse, Q-set, distribution grid and factor analysis process, although the methods of doing this may differ. However, Q researchers are able to decide which parts of the methodology fit with their position as a researcher. Some researchers, such as Jack Block and Stainton-Rogers, accept some and reject other particular characteristics of Q, based on their research positions.

Block (1924–2010) was a psychologist who made a major contribution to the field of personality development. He used Q-methodology to produce a way of conducting personality assessment. Participants were asked to order variables in reference to a designated personality type (Block, 1978: 5; Brown, 1997). Block (1978) viewed Q-methodology as a means of gaining 'impressions and personality formations of the observer' (p. 5). Block viewed his participants in the traditional positivist sense as instruments in research. Stephenson and Block had similar reasons for using Q as a form of assessment within their psychological research, but while Block acknowledged the benefits of asking participants to conduct Q-sorts subjectively, he tried to analyse his findings objectively, in contrast to Stephenson's throughgoing subjective stance (Brown, 1997).

Wendy Stainton-Rogers works in the field of health and is a social constructionist in postmodern research, producing Q research that has included a focus on the notion of 'addiction' (Stainton-Rogers and Stainton-Rogers, 1990). Influenced by Brown's research on behaviour, she was encouraged to use Q by the need to produce data on shared attitudes. Stainton-Rogers says that 'in Q [we] discovered such a means for exploring a whole plethora of images, ideas, debates and explanations' (Stainton-Rogers and Stainton-Rogers, 1990: 1). However, as a social constructionist, she was not interested in individual Q-sets, but in the differentiation between participants' viewpoints (Stainton-Rogers and Stainton-Rogers, 1990). Stainton-Rogers does not follow Stephenson's interest in subjectivity, and instead sees problems with a focus on self-reference, as she believes individuals can lie and deceive researchers concerning their true positions.

Overview of Q-methodology

Q-methodology is typically used to explore participants' perspectives on the research topic. Participants are presented with statements about the research topic with which they are likely to agree or disagree to a greater or lesser extent. The researcher constructs a concourse of a wide range of statements that might be sourced from a literature review, focus groups or expert knowledge. Statements can be 'opinions, plans, questions, options or strategies' (Eden et al., 2005). From this concourse of all possible relevant issues, a subset of specific statements to be sorted will be selected; this is known as the Q-set. Each statement is given a unique identifying number.

We often use personal statements that include pronouns such as 'I' or 'my' to emphasise to the participant that it is their perspective that we are seeking to investigate. Brown et al. (2018) is a recent study we conducted with some young people that included the following Q-set statements, which demonstrate how using this personal approach and careful age-appropriate wording of the statements can make them relatable and accessible:

- I have found the Explore University taster sessions helpful.

- University is good for lots of people, but not in my case.

- I can't wait to start uni.

- My family really wants me to go to uni.

INDIVIDUAL/GROUP TASK

Consider your own recent study and the literature you have read in this field. Write up to five statements that represent differing perspectives on your particular subject.

The process of sorting the statements is known as completing a Q-sort, and participants typically sort the statements onto a quasi-normal distribution grid (which is a reversed pyramid shape). Participants place those statements on which they have no strong position in the middle of the grid, to indicate that they have low saliency. Those on the extreme points of the grid are statements with high saliency (either strongly agreeable or disagreeable statements) to that participant. This form of distribution is known as a 'forced distribution', as it forces participants to compare and contrast the statements so they fit into a fixed pattern. Some qualitative researchers disagree with this approach, and prefer to allow each participant to lay the statements out howsoever they wish (Watts and Stenner, 2012). While you are still gaining familiarity with Q-methodology, we strongly recommend you follow the practice of using a defined distribution grid, because without one you will be unable to use software such as PQMethod to analyse your data.

The number of statements in the Q-set and the shape of the distribution grid are important design decisions for any Q study. Most studies usually have between 40 and 80 statements and have an 11- to 13-point scale on the distribution grid, from either −5 to +5 or −6 to +6 (Watts and Stenner, 2012). However, it is vital that the age of the participants is considered in the design. We often use fewer statements and a smaller distribution grid for young participants. An example of this is the recent study we completed for the Headstart Project (see https://bit.ly/2Dm6YM4). The study investigated young people's perspectives on experiences in their lives related to their resilience (without specifically mentioning the word resilience due to the complexity in its definition). In total, 35 young people (aged 9–16 years) sorted 40 statements onto a distribution grid that had a nine-point scale from −4 to +4. The Explore University project mentioned earlier in the chapter had 41 young people sorting 36 statements onto a distribution grid with a seven-point scale from −3 to +3. It is also possible to use images instead of text statements (e.g. Lobinger and Brantner, 2015), and this might be a useful approach to complete Q-sorts with younger children (e.g. to explore their views on concepts such as friendship or bullying).

The positions of the cards relative to each other in the completed Q-sort are recorded and the data are typically entered into a computer program such as PQMethod (downloadable for free at: http://schmolck.

org/qmethod/#PQMethod) for factorial analysis. In conducting their analysis, Q researchers may decide to focus predominantly on the factor analysis statistics, or may use them sparsely and instead write qualitative factor interpretations, depending on their positionality as a researcher. Describing the complicated processes of factor analysis in Q-methodology is outside the scope of this chapter; for a detailed explanation, we recommend reading Watts and Stenner (2012). This analysis stage is typically followed by another form of data collection method such as interviews or focus groups to further explore and triangulate the results of the Q-sorts.

Performing Q-sorts with young participants

To ensure young participants fully understand what is required of them, it can be effective to complete their Q-sort in a structured series of steps, rather than giving them a number of instructions and leaving them to 'get on with it', as might be done with adults. Watts and Stenner (2012) suggest that this type of structured approach can support the effective completion of the Q-sort by participants of all ages.

We begin by giving the participant the Q-set statement cards, and we ask them to sort them into three groups:

- statements with which they agree;

- statements with which they disagree; and

- statements they are unsure about or do not strongly care about.

Participants are told that there are no right or wrong answers; it is just their opinion we want. They are also told to be sure to ask us to explain any statements they may be unsure about. Once they have three groups, we ask them to focus on those with which they agree, and to spread them out on the tabletop, with the ones they most agree with on the right and those that they feel less strongly about towards the middle and left. Note that they have not yet been given the distribution grid at this time, only the cards.

Once they are happy with this initial sorting of the statements with which they agree, we provide them with the distribution grid,

Figure 14.1 Image of Q-sort

and explain how it works, including the condition of instruction. Participants are asked to place all the statements they agree with onto the right-hand side of the grid. The process is then repeated for the two remaining groups. First, those statements with which they disagree are placed on the left-hand side, and finally those they have no strong feelings about are used to 'fill up' the remaining spaces in the middle. While it might be thought desirable to have a balanced Q-set that you believe contains equal numbers of 'positive' or negative' statements, this is not necessary as each of your participants will have different perspectives, and it is not uncommon to have more statements in the agree group than the disagree group. This is not a problem as it will be the relative positions of the statements on the grid that are important.

Once all the statements are on the grid, we ask some probing questions to check that the placement of the statements matches the participant's intent. For example, 'I see you placed statement X in the +4 column and statement Y in the +3 column. Does that mean you agreed more with statement X or more with statement Y?' We also ask them to look at each statement and consider if it is the correct column or needs to be swapped with a neighbour. Once the participant is happy, the Q-sort is complete and can be recorded.

Early Years Pupil Premium study

A recent study was completed by Zeta Brown that investigated practitioners' perspectives on the Early Years Pupil Premium (EYPP) in England (Brown, 2018). This demonstrates how it is possible to use Q within a tight timescale and with a large number of participants at the same time. The research questions were:

- What are practitioners' perspectives on the EYPP funding?

- Is EYPP effective according to practitioners' perspectives, and does it 'close the gap' for disadvantaged children?

The project investigated the perspectives of 20 owners and managers of 19 settings in one local authority. The study sought to identify shared perspectives across the participants on this funding, including if they shared similar views on the EYPP's application and eligibility criteria. The interpretivist qualitative focus of the study was on the participants' positions, acknowledging that these positions can alter over time and can be dependent on situational circumstances.

The concourse (set of statements) was derived from a focus group with the local authorities 'Good to Outstanding' group. This generated a Q-set (34 statements in total) that was taken to the same group for respondent validation before being used in the project's main data collection. Example statements include:

- The funding is essential to support children's development.

- All children from low-income families need this funding.

- Some looked-after children miss out because the adoptive parents don't declare their status.

The Q-sort data collection was done during an LA Private, Voluntary and Independent (PVI) sector senior leadership update meeting. Attendees were asked if they wanted to take part in the project and provided time (30 minutes) during this update to be part of the research. There were approximately 50 attendees at the update (all owners/managers); 24 decided to take part in the study, and 20 successfully completed the card sort and were included in the analysis.

The project used the PQMethod software to analyse the data. In this study, centroid analysis was used to extract factors for varimax rotation. The study retained factors that had an eigenvalue (strength of that factor in relation to others) of 1.00 or higher.

In total, three factors were kept for interpretive analysis, and are briefly detailed below. The factors in this study represent 19 of the 20 practitioners included in the analysis. This is because one participant's perspectives did not load on any one factor. The numbers in brackets that appear throughout the following factor interpretations – e.g. (12; –3) – indicate where a particular statement (number 12) was placed on the grid (column –3) by that particular factor.

Factor 1: 'There are limitations to the EYPP funding; the application process has got to change'

The amount of variance accounted for is 35% and its eigenvalue is 6.9225. In total, eight practitioners held these communalities in their positions.

These practitioners held strong perspectives on the EYPP. Their position was interestingly not influenced by government objectives (12; –3), but they focused on highlighting the limitations of the funding by its application process. These practitioners state that it is not easy to access the funding (9; –4). They believe that it is a struggle to get parents to complete the online form (27; +4). They would prefer instead to apply for the funding on behalf of children in their care (28; +3) and would like more autonomy themselves to allocate the funding to children who really need it (4; +3). This group strongly stated that they get the funding too late in the academic year (7; +4). However, they do state that they have children who are not eligible for this funding but would benefit from it (30; +3).

Factor 2: 'The EYPP funding is beneficial, but it is not accessible to all who need it'

The amount of variance accounted for is 6% and its eigenvalue is 1.2481. In total, seven participants held these communalities in their positions. These participants worked mostly in nurseries; they are mostly managers at these settings, and all had over 10 years' experience.

Importantly, these participants declared that they had not been responsible for allocating this funding in their setting (26; −3). As with factor 1, they did not believe the funding could be better spent elsewhere (15; −3) and they highlighted difficulties in the application process. They also believe that the funding would be better used if they could allocate it to children whom they feel really need it (4; +3). What appeared more important for these practitioners were the eligibility criteria. They strongly agreed that they had children who were not eligible for this funding but would benefit from it (30; +4). They stated that they do not always know how to use the funding for each child (3; −3) and they find it difficult to decide how to use the funding if the child has no developmental delay (33; +3).

Factor 3: 'The EYPP funding has application and eligibility issues, but it is essential funding – it can support "eligible" children's development and others in the setting'

The amount of variance accounted for is 7% and its eigenvalue is 1.3709. In total, four practitioners held these communalities in their positions. These participants mostly worked in nurseries, were managers and those who stated had over 12 years' experience.

These practitioners strongly believe that the funding is essential to support children's development (1; +3) and they strongly state that the funding could not be better spent elsewhere (15; −4). They also believe that the government gives clear guidance on how to use the funding (18; −3).

Similarly to factors 1 and 2, they strongly agree that they get the funding too late in the academic year (7; +4). They believe that it is a struggle to get parents to complete the online form (27; +3) and they disagree that parents and carers are involved in how they use the funding (2; −3). They would prefer to apply for the funding on behalf of children in their care (28; +4). In contrast to factor 1, they strongly disagree that they have children in their setting who are eligible for this funding but have not received it (29; −4). Importantly, they use the funding for group activities that benefit more than one child (6; +3).

Conclusions from this study

The findings showed that the EYPP funding is clearly not working for these participants. There were consistent issues mentioned that included the application process and eligibility criteria. The use of Q-methodology meant that the findings were able to show the complexities and communalities among the participants' positions. They did not produce one factor that represented all of their perspectives, even though they all hold leadership roles.

A strength of the project was that it accessed the perspectives of practitioners in 19 differing settings. The time allocated for this data collection at the senior leadership meeting was limited to 30 minutes, and the use of Q-methodology meant that the project could gain detailed data from all who wanted to participate in this time frame. However, there were difficulties in collecting the data in this way. Sorting cards onto a forced distribution grid can be difficult, especially if it is not something that the participants have experienced before. There were local authority staff supporting the data collection; however, some prospective participants decided not to participate, and there were some participants that had to be removed because they had completed the task incorrectly (e.g. statements placed outside the confines of the distribution grid). It would have been advantageous to have been able to spend time with the individual participants to support the Q-sort and also ask additional interview questions. Similarly, post-Q-sort interviews after data analysis would have increased the qualitative data in the study. As with most education research, time was limited, but this study shows that Q-methodology can generate detailed qualitative data in short time frames.

Additional strengths of using Q-methodology

- The way Q-methodology is used often (in our experience) develops findings that we were not expecting. In this study, the researcher was not expecting such strong perspectives on the use of the EYPP that consistently showed barriers in its practical implementation.

- This study also used report sheets where participants were asked to briefly explain why they had placed statements in the most extreme distribution columns. This information further increased the qualitative data in the study, and these quotes were added to the factor interpretations in the study's publication (Brown, 2018).

■ In this study, the concourse (set of statements) was derived from a focus group with the local authorities 'Good to Outstanding' group. This meant that practitioners developed the relevant statements on the EYPP. These statements were then taken back to the same group and checked. The group also completed the card sort as a pilot study to further support the validity of the study.

Further limitations of using Q-methodology

■ Q-methodology focuses on investigating complexities and commonalities across a sample of participants. It is left to the researcher to decide whether they want to focus on collective perspectives. If they want to also focus on individual perspectives, additional research methods (such as report sheets and interviews) need to be added to increase the qualitative data gained from each participant.

■ It takes time to understand how to analyse Q data. There are some helpful resources available that have been cited in this chapter (e.g. Watts and Stenner, 2012). However, readers thinking of using Q need to ensure that they dedicate time to understanding the factor analysis process.

Summary

Q-methodology offers a full methodology for conducting research that can explore complex views. Depending on their positionality, researchers can select various complementary tools, and there are different ways to interpret the wealth of data produced by a software tool such as PQMethod. Q is suitable for use with young participants providing care is taken to consider the use of language and concepts being explored. Q can be used to collect data from a number of participants within a short time frame.

Glossary

Communality The amount of variance that a completed Q-sort shares with other participants' completed Q-sorts. Typically, Q-sorts with a high communality will load on the same factor.

Eigenvalue This number is calculated as the sum of the squared factor loadings for a factor. Dividing the eigenvalue by the number of Q-sorts in the study and multiplying by 100 will produce the variance accounted for by the factor. The eigenvalue is often used to decide whether a factor is significant to the study, with factors having eigenvalues of less than 1.00 typically being discarded.

Factor interpretation A written description of a factor, based on the positions of statements for the factor. This helps readers to understand the complexities of the participants' perspectives, and what the factor 'means'.

Loading Where one or more participants' completed Q-sorts share similar configurations of statements that closely relate to a factor, they are said to 'load' on that factor.

Q-set The complete set of statements to be sorted. Collectively, these should be broadly representative of possible views on the topic being investigated so that participants can express their opinions.

Q-sort The final configuration of the Q-set statements as produced by a participant who has completed sorting the cards onto the distribution grid.

Variance The range of opinions found within the Q-sort data. The amount of variance that a factor explains helps us to understand the significance of that factor (typically, the higher the variance explained, the more important the factor will be to the overall group of participants).

Varimax rotation A computer algorithm designed to present the Q-sort data results in a way that maximises the amount of variance explained by the factors.

Recommended reading

Brown, S. (1994–1995) Q methodology as the foundation for a science of subjectivity. *Operant Subjectivity*, 18: 1–16.

Brown, S. (1997) *The History and Principles of Q Methodology in Psychology and the Social Sciences*. Available at: www.scribd.com/document/92246042/History-and-Principles-of-Q-Steven-Brown (accessed 30 August 2018).

Watts, S. and Stenner, P. (2012) *Doing Q Methodological Research: Theory, Method and Interpretation*. London: Sage.

References

Basit, T. (2010) *Conducting Research in Educational Contexts.* London: Continuum.

Block, J. (1978) *The Q-Sort Method in Personality Assessment and Psychiatric Research.* Springfield, IL: Charles C. Thomas.

Brown, S. (1991–1992) *A Q Methodological Tutorial.* Available at: http://facstaff. uww.edu/cottlec/QArchive/Primer1.html (accessed 30 August 2018).

Brown, S. (1994–1995) Q methodology as the foundation for a science of subjectivity. *Operant Subjectivity,* 18: 1–16.

Brown, S. (1996) Q methodology and qualitative research. *Qualitative Health Research,* 6(4): 561–567.

Brown, S. (1997) *The History and Principles of Q Methodology in Psychology and the Social Sciences.* Available at: www.scribd.com/document/92246042/ History-and-Principles-of-Q-Steven-Brown (accessed 30 August 2018).

Brown, Z. (2018) *Good in Theory, Bad in Practice: Practitioner's Perspectives on the Early Years Pupil Premium in England,* doi: 10.1080/03004430.2018.1536049.

Brown, Z., Rhoades, G. and Smith, M. (2018) *Aspiring to Higher Education? The Complex Views of Secondary Students.* Paper presented at British Education Studies Association Conference: Internationalisation and Collaboration – Values and Value in Globalised Education, 28–29 June 2018. Available at: https://educationstudies.org.uk/?p=9101 (accessed 3 September 2018).

Cohen, L., Manion, L. and Morrison, K. (2007) *Research Methods in Education.* London: Routledge.

Eden, S., Donaldson, A. and Walker, G. (2005) Structuring subjectivities? Using Q methodology in human geography. *Area,* 37(4): 413–422.

Goldman, I. (1999) Q methodology as process and context in interpretivism, communication and psychoanalytic psychotherapy research. *The Psychological Record,* 49: 589–604.

Lobinger, K. and Brantner, C. (2015) Likable, funny or ridiculous? A Q-sort study on audience perceptions of visual portrayals of politicians. *Visual Communication,* 14: 15–40.

Rhoades, G. and Brown, Z. (2019) Q-methodology: the science of subjectivity. In M. Lambert (ed.), *Practical Research Methods in Education: An Early Researcher's Critical Guide.* London: Routledge, pp. 88–102.

Stainton-Rogers, R. and Stainton-Rogers, W. (1990) What the Brits get out of Q – and why their work may not line up with the American way of getting into it! *The Electronic Journal of Communication,* 1(1): 1–11.

Watts, S. and Stenner, P. (2012) *Doing Q Methodological Research: Theory, Method and Interpretation.* London: Sage.

Index

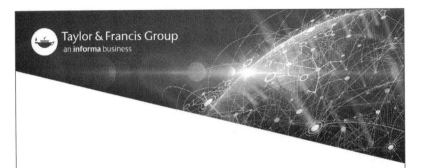

Taylor & Francis Group
an **informa** business

Taylor & Francis eBooks

www.taylorfrancis.com

A single destination for eBooks from Taylor & Francis
with increased functionality and an improved user
experience to meet the needs of our customers.

90,000+ eBooks of award-winning academic content in
Humanities, Social Science, Science, Technology, Engineering,
and Medical written by a global network of editors and authors.

TAYLOR & FRANCIS EBOOKS OFFERS:

A streamlined
experience for
our library
customers

A single point
of discovery
for all of our
eBook content

Improved
search and
discovery of
content at both
book and
chapter level

REQUEST A FREE TRIAL
support@taylorfrancis.com

Routledge
Taylor & Francis Group

CRC Press
Taylor & Francis Group